D1013546

A Day at a Time

A Day at a Time

A Day at a Time

Daily Reflections for Recovering People

HAZELDEN®

Hazelden
Center City, Minnesota 55012-0176

©1989 by Hazelden Foundation
All rights reserved. First published by
Hazelden Foundation 1994 (originally
published by CompCare Publishers 1989)
Printed in the United States of America
No portion of this publication may be
reproduced in any manner without the
written permission of the publisher

ISBN-13: 978-1-56838-036-0
ISBN-10: 1-56838-036-4

Editor's note

Hazelden offers a variety of information on chemical dependency and related areas. Our publications do not necessarily represent Hazelden's programs, nor do they officially speak for any Twelve Step organization.

The Twelve Steps and the Twelve Traditions of AA are reprinted with permission of Alcoholics Anonymous World Services, Inc. Permission to reprint the Twelve Steps and the Twelve Traditions of Alcoholics Anonymous does not mean that Alcoholics Anonymous has reviewed or approved the contents of this publication, nor that AA agrees with the views expressed herein. The views expressed herein are solely those of the author. AA is a program of recovery from alcoholism. Use of the Twelve Steps in connection with programs and activities that are patterned after AA, but which address other problems, does not imply otherwise.

Editor's Foreword

These daily reflections, prayers, and tags of memory-sticking phrases are intended to offer inspiration, comfort, and, above all, hope to those recovering from alcoholism, or from other forms of chemical dependency or compulsive behavior.

The book is based on the solid spiritual foundation of Alcoholics Anonymous (AA), and upon the Twelve Steps and Twelve Traditions. It draws also upon the great body of accumulated human wisdom—from civilization's Golden Age to our not-always-so-golden modern era, from Socrates to Bill W., co-founder of AA. Here, in brief day-by-day messages are some of these available riches, the words of poets, scholars, philosophers, psychologists, which are the verbal sums of centuries of human experience. May those sums and sayings serve as guidelines—a day at a time.

Reflection for the Day

In the old days, I saw everything in terms of *forever*. Endless hours were spent rehashing old mistakes. I tried to take comfort in the forlorn hope that tomorrow "would be different."

As a result, I lived a fantasy life in which happiness was all but nonexistent. No wonder I rarely smiled and hardly ever laughed aloud. *Do I still think in terms of "forever"?*

Today I Pray

May I set my goals for the New Year not at the year-long mark, but one day at a time. My traditional New Year's resolutions have been so grandly stated and so soon broken. Let me not weaken my resolve by stretching it to cover "forever"—or even one long year. May I reapply it firmly each new day. May I learn not to stamp my past mistakes with that indelible word, "forever." Instead, may each single day in each New Year be freshened by my new-found hope.

Today I Will Remember

Happy New Day.

Reflection for the Day

Before I came to the Program, I hadn't the faintest idea of what it was to "Live In The Now." I often became obsessed with the things that happened yesterday, last week, or even five years ago. Worse yet, many of my waking hours were spent clearing away the "wreckage of the future." "To me," Walt Whitman once wrote, "every hour of the day and night is an unspeakably perfect miracle." *Can I truly believe that in my heart?*

Today I Pray

Let me carry only the weight of 24 hours at one time, without the extra bulk of yesterday's regrets or tomorrow's anxieties. Let me breathe the blessings of each new day for itself, by itself, and keep my human burdens contained in daily perspective. May I learn the balance of soul that comes through keeping close to God.

Today I Will Remember

Don't borrow from tomorrow.

Reflection for the Day

My addiction is three-fold in that it affects me physically, mentally, and spiritually. As a chemically dependent person, I was totally out of touch not only with myself, but with reality. Day after miserable day, like a caged animal on a treadmill, I repeated my self-destructive pattern of living. *Have I begun to break away from my old ideas? Just for today, can I adjust myself to what is, rather than try to adjust everything to my own desires?*

Today I Pray

I pray that I may not be caught up again in the downward, destructive spiral which removed me from myself and from the realities of the world around me. I pray that I may adjust to people and situations as they are instead of always trying, unsuccessfully and with endless frustration, to bend them to my own desires.

Today I Will Remember

I can only change myself.

JANUARY 4

Reflection for the Day

For a good part of my life, I saw things mostly in negative terms. *Everything* was serious, heavy, or just plain awful. Perhaps now I can truly change my attitude, searching out the winners in the Program who have learned how to live comfortably in the real world—without numbing their brains with mood-altering chemicals. *If things get rough today, can I take a quiet moment and say to myself, as the philosopher Homer once said, "Bear patiently, my heart—for you have suffered heavier things..."?*

Today I Pray

May the peace of God that passes all human understanding fill the place within me that once harbored my despair. May an appreciation for living—even for life's trails—cancel out my old negative attitudes. During heart-heavy moments, help to remind me that my heart was once much heavier still.

Today I Will Remember

I, too, am a winner.

Reflection for the Day

"Vision is, I think, the ability to make good estimates," wrote Bill W., the co-founder of Alcoholics Anonymous. "Some might feel this sort of striving to be heresy against 'One Day At A Time.' But that valuable principle really refers to our mental and emotional lives, and means chiefly that we are not foolishly to repine over the past nor wishfully daydream about the future." *Can I believe that "A day has a hundred pockets when one has much to put in them..."?*

Today I Pray

I pray that the bright colors of this day may not be blurred by muted vagaries of the future or dulled by storm-gray remnants from the past. I pray that my Higher Power will help me to choose my actions and concerns out of the wealth of busyness that each day offers.

Today I Will Remember

I will not lose for today,
If I choose for today.

Reflection for the Day

"As individuals and as a fellowship," Bill W. continued, "we shall surely suffer if we cast the whole idea of planning for tomorrow into a fatuous idea of providence. God's real providence has endowed us human beings with a considerable capability for foresight, and He evidently expects us to use it. Of course, we shall often miscalculate the future in whole or in part, but that is better than to refuse to think at all." *Have I begun to believe that I am only an actor in a play which the Manager directs?*

Today I Pray

May I make prudent use of the foresight and power of choice which God has given me, to plan wisely, one Step at a time, without becoming a slave to apprehension, regret, or anxiety. I pray that God's will be done through the exercising of my own will, which He, in His goodness, has given me.

Today I Will Remember

God wills my will to be.

Reflection for the Day

I'm beginning to see just how unnatural my old life actually was, and that it became increasingly unnatural as my illness progressed. The longer I'm in the Program, the more natural this new way of life seems. At first, it was impossible for me to extend my hand to a newcomer; such an act was wholly unnatural for me. But it is becoming increasingly easier for me to reach out to another person. Sharing my experience, strength, and hope is becoming a natural part of daily living. *Have I learned that I can't keep what I've gotten unless I "give it away"? Will I take the time to share today?*

Today I Pray

May I share my love, my joy, my happiness, my time, my hospitality, my knowledge of things on earth, and my faith in a Higher Power. Even though I may not see the results of my acts of sharing, my I take joy in the acts themselves. May sharing, according to God's plan, become as natural to me as speaking or breathing.

Today I Will Remember

Be never sparing in caring and sharing.

Reflection for the Day

Today is the day for which I asked and for which I have been given strength. That in itself is a miracle. In my old life, I constantly endangered myself as well as countless others. So the very fact that I am alive is the great miracle from which all other miracles will flow, providing I continue to do the things that have brought me this far in my new life. *Am I grateful that I have been given this day?*

Today I Pray

May God's goodness and mercy follow me all the days of my life. May I never cease to wonder at the greatest miracle in my life—that I am alive, here, on this green earth, and growing healthier with the life-preserving tools I have been given. Since God has chosen to give me life and to preserve my life, even through the dangers of addiction, may I always continue to listen for His plan for me. May I always believe in miracles.

Today I Will Remember

My life is a miracle.

Reflection for the Day

In the past, and sometimes even now, I automatically have thought, "Why *me*?", when I'm trying to learn that my first problem is to accept my present circumstances as they are, myself as I am, and the people around me as they are. Just as I finally accepted my powerlessness over my addiction, so must I accept my powerlessness over people, places, and things. *Am I learning to accept life on life's terms?*

Today I Pray

May I learn to control my urge to control, my compulsion to manage, neaten, organize, and label the lives of others. May I learn to accept situations and people as they are instead of as I would like them to be. Thus, may I do away with the ongoing frustrations that a controlling person, by nature, faces continually. May I be entirely ready to have God remove this defect of character.

Today I Will Remember

Control for the controller (me).

Reflection for the Day

Since I came to the Program, I've become increasingly aware of the Serenity Prayer. I see it on literature covers, the walls of meeting rooms, and in the homes of new-found friends. "God grant me the serenity to accept the things I cannot change, the courage to change the things I can, and the wisdom to know the difference." *Do I understand the Serenity Prayer? Do I believe in its power and repeat it often? Is it becoming easier for me to accept the things I cannot change?*

Today I Pray

God grant that the words of the Serenity Prayer never become mechanical for me or lose their meaning in the lulling rhythms of repetition. I pray that these words will continue to take on new depths of significance as I fit life's realities to them. I trust that I may find the solutions I need in this prayer, which, in its simplicity, encompasses all of life's situations.

Today I Will Remember

Share the prayer.

Reflection for the Day

The experiences of thousands upon thousands of people have proven that acceptance and faith are capable of producing freedom from dependence on chemicals. When we apply the same principles of acceptance and faith to our emotional problems, however, we discover that only relative results are possible. Obviously, for example, nobody can ever become completely free from fear, anger, or pride. None of us will ever achieve perfect love, harmony, or serenity. We'll have to settle for very gradual progress, punctuated occasionally by very heavy setbacks. *Have I begun to abandon my old attitude of "all or nothing"?*

Today I Pray

May God grant me the patience to apply those same principles of faith and acceptance which are keys to my recovery to the whole of my emotional being. May I learn to recognize the festering of my own human anger, my hurt, my frustration, my sadness. With the help of God, may I find appropriate ways to deal with these feelings without doing harm to myself or others.

Today I Will Remember

Feelings are facts.

Reflection for the Day

When I sit quietly and compare my life today with the way it used to be, the difference is almost beyond belief. But things aren't always rosy; some days are a lot better than others. I tend to accept the bad days more easily on an intellectual level than I do emotionally, or at gut-level. There are no pat answers, but part of the solution surely lies in a constant effort to practice all of the Twelve Steps. *Do I accept the fact that my Higher Power will never give me more than I can handle—one day at a time?*

Today I Pray

That I may receive strength in the knowledge that God never gives us more than we can bear, that I can always, somehow, endure present pain, whereas the trials of a lifetime, condensed into one disasterous moment, would surely overcome me. Thanks be to God for giving us only those tribulations which are in proportion to our strength, never destroying us in our frailty. May I remember that fortitude grows out of suffering.

Today I Will Remember

Present pain is endurable.

Reflection for the Day

The Program and my friends in the fellowship have provided me with a whole new set of tools for living. Even the slogans that once seemed so trite and corny are now becoming an important part of my daily life: Easy Does It; First Things First; This, Too, Will Pass. If I use all of my tools regularly and well, they'll also help rid me of such negative feelings as guilt, anxiety, rebellion, and pride. *When I'm feeling depressed, do I use the tools that have been proven effective? Or do I grit my teeth and suffer in painful silence?*

Today I Pray

I praise my wonder-working Higher Power for giving me the tools for recovery, once I admitted I was powerless over my addiction and gave myself over to the will of God as I understand Him. I give thanks for the Twelve Steps, and for the fellowship of the group, which can help me see myself honestly. I give thanks for those words and phrases which become, as we understand them more completely, banners in our celebration of sobriety.

Today I Will Remember

Pass on the passwords to recovery.

Reflection for the Day

I admitted that I couldn't win the booze and chemical battle on my own. So I finally began to accept the critically important fact that dependence on a Higher Power could help me achieve what had always seemed impossible. I stopped running. I stopped fighting. For the first time, I began accepting. And for the first time, I began to be really free. *Do I realize that it doesn't matter what kind of shoes I'm wearing when I'm running away?*

Today I Pray

May I know the freedom that comes with surrender to a Higher Power—that most important kind of surrender that means neither "giving in" nor "giving up" but "giving over" my will to the will of God. Like a weary fugitive from spiritual order, may I stop hiding, dodging, running. May I find peace in surrender, in the knowledge that God wills that I be whole and healthy and He will show me the way.

Today I Will Remember

First surrender, then serenity.

Reflection for the Day

I must never forget who and what I am and where I come from. I have to remember the nature of my illness and what it was like before I came to the Program. I'll try to keep the memory green, yet not spend my time dwelling morbidly on the past. I won't be afraid to enjoy what is beautiful, and to believe that as I give to others, so others will give to me. *Can I ever afford to forget what it used to be like, even for one minute?*

Today I Pray

May I never forget the painful days of my addiction. May I never forget that the same misery awaits me if I should slip back into the old patterns. At the same time, may such backwards glances serve only to bolster my own present strength and the strength of others like me. Please, God, do not let me dredge up these recollections in order to outdo or "out-drunk" my fellow members. Like others who are chemically dependent, I must be wary of my desire to be center stage in the spotlight.

Today I Will Remember

I do more when I don't "outdo."

Reflection for the Day

When we first came to the Program, whether for ourselves or under pressure from others, some of us were all but sickened by the concept of "surrender." To admit to defeat flew in the face of our life-long beliefs. And so we secretly vowed, at first, that the very idea of surrender was unthinkable. *Have I truly come to believe that only through utter defeat am I able to take the first step toward liberation and strength? Or do I still harbor reservations about the principle of "letting go and letting God..."?*

Today I Pray

May I really believe that the complete surrender of my whole being to a Higher Power is the way to serenity. For I can be whole only in Him, who has the power to make me whole. May I do away with any feelings of wanting to "hold out" and never admit defeat. May I unlearn the old adage which tells me that I must "never give up" and realize that such pridefulness could keep me from recovery.

Today I Will Remember

From wholly His to whole.

Reflection for the Day

I have been told over and over that I must constantly work to give up my old ideas. "That's easy for you to say," I've sometimes thought. All my life, I have been programmed, computer-style; specific inputs brought forth predictable responses. My mind still tends to react as a computer reacts, but I am learning to destroy the old tapes and literally reprogram myself. *Am I fully willing to abandon my old ideas? Am I being fearless and thorough on a daily basis?*

Today I Pray

Help me to take inventory each day of my stock of my new, healthy thoughts, throwing out the old ones as I happen upon them without regret or nostalgia. For I have outgrown those old ideas, which are as scuffed and run-over as an old pair of shoes. Now, in the light, I can see that they are filled with holes.

Today I Will Remember

The Program reprograms.

Reflection for the Day

If we are determined to stop drinking or using other chemicals, there must be no reservations whatsoever, nor any lurking notion that our allergy of the body and obsession of the mind will someday reverse themselves. Our regeneration comes through the splendid paradox of the Twelve Steps: Strength arises from complete defeat, and the loss of one's old life is a condition for finding a new one. *Am I convinced that in powerlessness, power comes? Am I certain that by releasing my life and will I am released?*

Today I Pray

May I know power through powerlessness, victory through surrender, triumph through defeat. May I learn to relinquish any trace of secret pride that I can "do it by myself." Let my will be absorbed and steered by the omnipotent will of God.

Today I Will Remember

Let go and let God.

Reflection for the Day

It was far easier for me to accept my powerlessness over my addiction than it was for me to accept the notion that some sort of Higher Power could accomplish that which I had been unable to accomplish myself. Simply by seeking help and accepting the fellowship of others similarly afflicted, the craving left me. And I realized that if I was doing what I was powerless alone to do, then surely I was doing so by some Power outside my own and obviously greater. *Have I surrendered my life into the hands of God?*

Today I Pray

May God erase in me the arrogant pride which keeps me from listening to Him. May my unhealthy dependence on chemicals and my clinging dependence on those nearby be transformed into reliance on God. Only in this kind of dependency/reliance on a Higher Power will I find my own transformation.

Today I Will Remember

I am God-dependent.

Reflection for the Day

The first psychiatrist to recognize the work of Alcoholics Anonymous, Dr. Harry Tiebout, used many concepts of the Program in his own practice. Over many years, the doctor's study of the "conversion experience" led him to see, first, that it is the act of surrender which initiates the switch from negative to positive; second, that the positive phase is really a *state* of surrender which follows the act of surrender; and third, that the state of surrender, if maintained, supplies an emotional tone to all thinking and feeling that ensures healthy adjustment. *Am I living in a constant state of surrender?*

Today I Pray

May I understand that I do not have to "unlearn" my respect for "self-reliance," that trait of character which I heard praised so often from the time I was a tiny child. Only my understanding of the word must change. For as I come to know that "self" is part of God, that I am nothing except in His Being, there is no quarrel between self-reliance and God-reliance. May I rely upon that self which is God's.

Today I Will Remember

Not part-god, but part of God.

Reflection of the Day

Every person, no matter what his or her balance for good or evil, is a part of the Divine economy. We are all children of God, and it is unlikely that He intends to favor one over another. So it is necessary for all of us to accept whatever positive gifts we receive with a deep humility, always bearing in mind that our negative attitudes were first necessary as a means of reducing us to such a state that we would be ready for a gift of the positive ones via the conversation experience. *Do I accept the fact that my addiction and the bottom I finally reached are the bedrock upon which my spiritual foundation rests?*

Today I Pray

May I know that from the first moment I admitted my powerlessness, God-given power was mine. Every step taken from that moment of defeat has been a step in the right direction. The First Step is a giant step. Through it is often taken in despair, may I realize that I must be drained of hope before I can be refilled with fresh hope, sapped of wilfulness before I can feel the will of God.

Today I Will Remember

Power through powerlessness.

Reflection for the Day

In a very real sense, we are imprisoned by our inability or unwillingness to reach out for help to a Power greater than ourselves. But in time, we pray to be relieved of the bondage of self, so that we can better do God's will. In the words of Ramakrishna, "The sun and moon are not mirrored in cloudy waters, thus the Almighty cannot be mirrored in a heart that is obsessed by the idea of 'me and mine.'" *Have I set myself free from the prison of self-will and pride which I myself have built? Have I accepted freedom?*

Today I Pray

May the word freedom take on new meanings for me, not just "freedom *from*" my addiction, but "freedom *to*" overcome it. Not just freedom *from* the slavery of self-will, but freedom *to* hear and carry out the will of God.

Today I Will Remember

Freedom *from* means freedom *to*.

Reflection for the Day

We must never be blinded by the futile philosophy that we are just the hapless victims of our inheritance, of our life experience, and of our surroundings—that these are the sole forces that make our decisions for us. This is not the road to freedom. We have to believe that we can really choose. As addictive persons, we lost our ability to choose whether we would pursue our addictions. Yet we finally did make choices that brought about our recovery. *Do I believe that in "becoming willing" I have made the best of all choices?*

Today I Pray

May I shed the idea that I am the world's victim, an unfortunate creature caught in a web of circumstance, inferring that others ought to "make it up to me" because I have been given a bad deal on this earth. We are always given choices. May God help me to choose wisely.

Today I Will Remember

God is not a puppeteer.

Reflection for the Day

Among the many gifts that we are offered in the Program is the gift of freedom. Paradoxically, however, the gift of freedom is not without a price tag; freedom can only be achieved by paying the price called *acceptance*. Similarly, if we can surrender to God's guidance, it will cost us our self-will, that "commodity" so precious to those of us who have always thought we could and should run the show. *Is my freedom today worth the price tag of acceptance?*

Today I Pray

May God teach me acceptance—the ability to accept the things I cannot change. God also grant me courage to change those things I can. God help me to accept the illness of my addiction and give me the courage to change my addictive behavior.

Today I Will Remember

Accept the addiction.
Change the behavior.

Reflection for the Day

Even with a growing understanding of the Program and its Twelve Steps, we sometimes might find it difficult to believe that our new way of life leads to personal freedom. Suppose, for example, I feel imprisoned in an uncomfortable job or troublesome personal relationship. What am I doing about it? In the past, my reflex reaction was to try to manipulate the things and people around me into being more acceptable to me. Today, I realize that happiness can't be won that way. *Am I learning that freedom from despair and frustration can come only from changing, in myself, the attitudes that are perpetuating the conditions that cause me grief?*

Today I Pray

May I be given clear eyes to see—and then to stop myself—when I am manipulating the lives of those around me, my daily associates, friends, family. May I always be aware that change must begin within myself.

Today I Will Remember

Change from the inside out.

Reflection for the Day

Personal freedom is mine for the taking. No matter how close are the ties of love and concern that bind me to my family and friends, I must always remember that I am an individual, free to be myself and live my own life in serenity and joy. The key word in this realization is *personal*. For I *can* free myself from many involvements that *seem* necessary. Through the Program, I am learning to develop my own personality. *Am I reinforcing personal freedom by leaving others free to control their actions and destinies?*

Today I Pray

May I find personal freedom, by reevaluating associations, establishing new priorities, gaining respect for my own personhood. May I give others equal room to find their own kinds of personal freedoms.

Today I Will Remember

Take the liberty; it's yours.

Reflection for the Day

I can attain real dignity, importance, and individuality only by a dependence on a Power which is great and good, beyond anything I can imagine or understand. I will try my utmost to use this power in making all my decisions. Even though my human mind cannot forecast what the outcome will be, I will try to be confident that whatever comes will be for my ultimate good. *Just for today, will I try to live this day only, and not tackle my whole life problem at once?*

Today I Pray

May I make no decision, engineer no change in the course of my lifestream, without calling upon my Higher Power. May I have faith that God's plan for me is better than any scheme I could devise for myself.

Today I Will Remember

God is the architect. I am the builder.

Reflection for the Day

Now that I am in the Program, I am no longer enslaved by alcohol and other drugs. Free, free at last from the morning-after tremors, the dry heaves, the three-day beard, the misplaced eyelashes. Free, free at last from working out the alibis and hoping they won't unravel; free from blackouts; free from watching the clock so that I can somehow get that desperately-needed "first one." *Do I treasure my freedom from chemical enslavement?*

Today I Pray

Praise God that I am free of chemicals. This is my first freedom, from which other freedoms will develop—freedom to appraise my behavior sanely and constructively, freedom to grow as a person, freedom to maintain relationships with others on a sound basis. I will never cease to thank my Higher Power for leading me away from my enslavement.

Today I Will Remember

Praise God for my freedom.

Reflection for the Day

I used to imagine my life as a grotesque abstract painting: a montage of crises framed by end-upon-end catastrophes. My days all were grey and my thoughts greyer still. I was haunted by dread and nameless fears. I was filled with self-loathing. I had no idea who I was, what I was, or why I was. I miss none of those feelings. Today, step by step, I am discovering myself and learning that I can be free to be me. *Am I grateful for my new life? Have I taken the time to thank God today for the fact that I am clean and sober—and alive?*

Today I Pray

May calm come to me after the turmoil and nightmares of the past. As my fears and self-hatred dissipate, may the things of the spirit replace them. For in the spiritual world, as in the material world, there is no empty space. May I be filled with the spirit of my Higher Power.

Today I Will Remember

Morning scatters nightmares.

Reflection for the Day

Have I gained freedom simply because one day I was weak and the next day I became suddenly strong? Have I changed from the helpless and hopeless person I once seemed to be simply by resolving, "from now on, things will be different..."? Is the fact that I am more comfortable today than ever before the result of my own will power? Can I take credit for pulling myself up by my own bootstraps? I know better, for I sought refuge in a Power greater than myself—a Power which is still beyond my ability to visualize. *Do I consider the change in my life a miracle far beyond the working of any human power?*

Today I Pray

As the days of sobriety lengthen, and the moment of decision becomes farther behind me, may I never lose sight of the Power that changed my life. May I remember that my sobriety is an ongoing miracle, not just a once-in-a-lifetime transformation.

Today I Will Remember

Life is an ongoing miracle.

Reflection for the Day

One of the most constructive things I can do is to learn to listen to myself and get in touch with my true feelings. For years, I tuned myself out, going along, instead, with what others felt and said. Even today, it sometimes seems that *they* have it all together, while I'm still stumbling about. Thankfully, I'm beginning to understand that people-pleasing takes many forms. Slowly but steadily, I've also begun to realize that it's possible for me to change my old patterns. *Will I encourage myself to tune in to the real me? Will I listen carefully to my own inner voice with the expectation that I'll hear some wonderful things?*

Today I Pray

I pray that I may respect myself enough to listen to my real feelings, those emotions which for so long I refused to hear or name or own, which festered in me like a poison. May I know that I need to stop often, look at my feelings, listen to the inner me.

Today I Will Remember

I will own my feelings.

Reflection for the Day

The longer I'm in the Program, the more clearly I see why it's important for me to understand *why* I do what I do, and say what I say. In the process, I'm coming to realize what kind of person I really am. I see now, for example, that it's far easier to be honest with other people than with myself. I'm learning, also, that we're all hampered by our need to justify our actions and words. *Have I taken an inventory of myself as suggested in the Twelve Steps? Have I admitted my faults to myself, to God, and to another human being?*

Today I Pray

May I not be stalled in my recovery process by the enormity of the Program's Fourth Step, taking a moral inventory of myself, or by admitting these shortcomings to myself, to God, and to another human being. May I know that honesty to myself about myself is all-important.

Today I Will Remember

I cannot mend if I bend the truth.

Reflection for the Day

Looking back, I realize just how much of my life has been spent in dwelling upon the faults of others. It provided much self-satisfaction, to be sure, but I see now just how subtle and actually perverse the process became. After all was said and done, the net effect of dwelling on the so-called faults of others was self-granted permission to remain comfortably unaware of my *own* defects. *Do I still point my finger at others and thus self-deceptively overlook my own shortcomings?*

Today I Pray

May I see that my preoccupation with the faults of others is really a smokescreen to keep me from taking a hard look at my own, as well as a way to bolster my own failing ego. May I check out the "why's" of my blaming.

Today I Will Remember

Blame-saying
Is game-playing.

Reflection for the Day

The Program enables us to discover two road-blocks that keep us from seeing the value and comfort of the spiritual approach: self-justification and self-righteousness. The first grimly assures me that I'm always right. The second mistakenly comforts me with the delusion that I'm better than other people—"holier than thou." *Just for today, will I pause abruptly while rationalizing and ask myself, "Why am I doing this? Is this self-justification really honest?"*

Today I Pray

May I overcome the need to be "always right" and know the cleansing feeling of release that comes with admitting, openly, a mistake. May I be wary of setting myself up as an example of self-control and fortitude, and give credit where it is due—to a Higher Power.

Today I Will Remember

To err is human, but I need to admit it.

Reflection for the Day

Rare is the recovering alcoholic who will now dispute the fact that *denial* is a primary symptom of the illness. The Program teaches us that alcoholism is the only illness which actually tells the afflicted person that he or she *really isn't sick at all.* Not surprisingly, then, our lives as practicing alcoholics were characterized by endless rationalization, countless alibis and, in short, a steadfast unwillingness to accept the fact that we were, without question, bodily and mentally different from our fellows. *Have I conceded to my innermost self that I am truly powerless over alcohol?*

Today I Pray

May the Program's First Step be not half-hearted for me, but a total admission of powerlessness over my addiction. May I rid myself of that first symptom—denial—which refuses to recognize any other symptom of my disease.

Today I Will Remember

Deny denial.

Reflection for the Day

If I am troubled, worried, exasperated, or frustrated, do I tend to rationalize the situation and lay the blame on someone else? When I am in such a state, is my conversation punctuated with, "*He* did. .", "*She* said...", "*They* did..."? Or can I honestly admit that perhaps I'm at fault. My peace of mind depends on overcoming my negative attitudes and tendency toward rationalization. *Will I try, day by day, to be rigorously honest with myself?*

Today I Pray

May I catch myself as I talk in the third person, "He did..." or "They promised..." or "She said she would..." and listen for the blaming that has become such a pattern for me and preserves delusion. May I do a turnabout and face myself instead.

Today I Will Remember

Honesty is the only policy.

Reflection for the Day

I used to be an expert at unrealistic self-appraisal. At certain times, I would look only at that part of my life which seemed good. Then I would magnify whatever real or imagined virtues I had attained. Next, I would pat myself on the back for the fantastic job I was doing in the Program. Naturally, this generated a craving for still more "accomplishments" and still greater approval. Wasn't that the pattern of my days during active addiction? The difference now, though, is that I can use the best alibi known—the spiritual alibi. *Do I sometimes rationalize willful actions and nonsensical behavior in the name of "spiritual objectives"?*

Today I Pray

God help me to know if I still crave attention and approval to the point of inflating my own virtues and magnifying my accomplishments in the Program or anywhere. May I keep a realistic perspective about my good points, even as I learn to respect myself.

Today I Will Remember

Learn to control inflation.

Reflection for the Day

Why do I do what I do? Why did I say what I said? Why on earth did I put off an important responsibility? Questions like these, best asked of myself in a quiet time of meditation, demand honest answers. I may have to think deeply for those answers, going beyond the tempting rationalizations that lack the luster of truth. *Have I accepted the fact that self-deception can only damage me, providing a clouded and unrealistic picture of the person I really am?*

Today I Pray

May God allow me to push aside my curtain of fibs, alibis, rationalizations, justifications, distortions, and downright lies and let in the light on the real truths about myself. May I meet the person I really am and take comfort in the person I can become.

Today I Will Remember

Hello, Me. Meet the real Me.

Reflection for the Day

When we first stopped drinking, using, overeating, or gambling, it was an enormous relief to find that the people we met in the Program seemed quite different than those apparently hostile masses we know as "They." We were met not with criticism and suspicion, but with understanding and concern. However, we still encounter people who get on our nerves, both within the Program and outside it. Obviously, we must begin to accept the fact that there *are* people who'll sometimes say things with which we disagree, or do things we don't like. *Am I beginning to see that learning to live with differences is essential to my comfort and, in turn, to my continuing recovery?*

Today I Pray

May I recognize that people's differences make our world go around and tolerate people who "rub me the wrong way." May I understand that I must give them room, that some of my hostile attitudes toward others may be leftovers from the unhealthy days when I tended to view others as mobilized against me.

Today I Will Remember

Learn to live with differences.

Reflection for the Day

The slogan "Live and Let Live" can be extremely helpful when we are having trouble tolerating other people's behavior. We know for certain that nobody's behavior—no matter how offensive, distasteful, or vicious—is worth the price of a relapse. Our own recovery is primary, and while we must be unafraid of walking away from people or situations that cause us discomfort, we must also make a special effort to try to understand other people—especially those who rub us the wrong way. *Can I accept the fact, in my recovery, that it is more important to understand than to be understood?*

Today I Pray

When I run headlong into someone's unpleasant behavior, may I first try my best to understand. Then, if my own sobriety seems threatened, may I have the courage to remove myself from the situation.

Today I Will Remember

Live and let live.

Reflection for the Day

Until now, we may have equated the idea of beginning again with a previous record of failure. This isn't necessarily so. Like students who finish grade school and begin again in high school, or workers who find new ways to use their abilities, our beginnings must not be tinged with a sense of failure. In a sense, every day is a time of beginning again. We need never look back with regret. Life is not necessarily like a blackboard that must be erased because we didn't solve problems correctly, but rather a blackboard that must be cleaned to make way for the new. *Am I grateful for all that has prepared me for this moment of beginning?*

Today I Pray

May I understand that past failures need not hamper my new courage or give a murky cast to my new beginnings. May I know, from the examples of others in the Program, that former failings, once faced and rectified, can be a more solid foundation for a new life than easy-come successes.

Today I Will Remember

Failings can be footings for recovery.

Reflection for the Day

I can always take strength and comfort from knowing I belong to a worldwide fellowship. Hundreds and hundreds of thousands, just like me are working together for the same purpose. None of us needs ever to be alone again, because each of us in our own way works for the good of others. We are bound together by a common problem that can be solved by love and understanding and mutual service. The Program—like the little wheel in the old hymn—runs by the grace of God. *Have I thanked God today for helping me to find the Program, which is showing me the way to a new life?*

Today I Pray

May my thanks be lifted to God each day for dispelling my self-inflicted loneliness, for warming my stoicism, for leading me to the boundless fund of friendship in the Program.

Today I Will Remember

I have a world of friends.

Reflection for the Day

I am grateful for my friends in the Program. Right now I am aware of the blessings of friendship—the blessings of meeting, of sharing, of smiling, of listening, and of being available when needed. Right now I know that if I want a friend, I must be a friend. *Will I vow, this day, to be a better friend to more people? Will I strive, this day—in my thoughts, words, and actions—to disclose the kind of friend I am?*

Today I Pray

May I restore in kind to the fellowship of the Program the friendship I have so hungrily taken from it. After years of glossing my lonely existence with superficial acquaintanceships, may I learn again the reciprocal joys of caring and sharing.

Today I Will Remember

Be a friend.

Reflection for the Day

We sometimes hear someone say, "He is standing in his own light." A mental picture then clearly reveals that many of us tend to shadow our own happiness by mistaken thinking. Let us learn to stand aside so the light can shine on us and all we do. For only then can we see ourselves and our circumstances with true clarity. With the Program and the Twelve Steps, we no longer need to stand in our own light and try alone to solve our problems in darkness. *When I am faced with a seemingly insoluble problem, will I ask myself if I am standing in my own light?*

Today I Pray

May I not get in my own way, obscure my own clarity of thought, stumble over my own feet, block my own doorway to recovery. If I find that I am standing in my own light, may I ask my Higher Power and my friends in the group to show me a new vantage point.

Today I Will Remember

If all I can see is my shadow, I'm in my own light.

Reflection for the Day

Today I will take the time to list the positive aspects of my new life and the blessings that accompany the miracles of my recovery. I will be grateful for the seemingly simple ability to eat normally, to fall asleep with a feeling of contentment, to awaken with a gladness to be alive. I will be grateful for the ability to face life on life's terms—with peace of mind, self-respect, and full possession of all my faculties. *On a daily basis, do I count my blessings? Do I seek through prayer and meditation to improve my conscious contact with God as I understand Him?*

Today I Pray

On this day of love-giving, may I count all the good things in my life and give thanks for them. May I take no blessing for granted, including the beating of my own heart and the fresh feel of new air as I breathe.

Today I Will Remember

To count—and consider—my blessings.

Reflection for the Day

When I become angry, can I admit to it and state it as a fact without allowing it to build up and burst out in inappropriate ways? Pent-up anger, I've finally begun to learn, quickly shatters the peace of mind that's so critical to my ongoing recovery. When I become enraged and lose control, I unwittingly hand over control to the person, place, or thing with which I am enraged. *When I'm angry will I try to remember that I am endangering myself? Will I "count to ten" by calling a friend in the Program and say the Serenity Prayer aloud?*

Today I Pray

May I recognize angry feelings and let them out a little at a time, stating my anger as a fact, instead of allowing it to fester into rage and explode uncontrollably.

Today I Will Remember

Anger is. Rage need not be.

Reflection for the Day

What about "justifiable anger"? If somebody cheats us or acts toward us in an outrageous manner, don't we have the *right* to be furious? The hard-learned experiences of countless others in the Program tell us that adventures in rage are usually extremely dangerous. So, while we must recognize anger enough to say "I am angry," we must not allow the build-up of rage, however justifiable. *Can I accept the fact that if I am to live, I have to be free of anger?*

Today I Pray

Even though I go out of the way to skirt them, may I be aware that there always will be certain situations or certain people who will make me angry. When my anger doesn't seem justifiable—with arguable reason behind it—I may deny it, even to myself. May I recognize my anger, whether it is reasonable or not, before I bury it alive.

Today I Will Remember

It is all right to feel anger.

Reflection for the Day

If I become angry today, I'll pause and *think* before I say anything, remembering that my anger can turn back upon me and worsen my difficulties. I'll try to remember, too, that well-timed silence can give me command of a stressful situation as angry reproaches *never* can. In such moments of stress, I'll remember that my power over others is nonexistent, and that only God is all-powerful. *Have I learned that I alone can destroy my own peace of mind?*

Today I Pray

May I learn that I can choose how to handle my anger—in silence or as a tantrum, a rage, a fist fight, a pillow fight, a tirade, an elaborate plan to "get back at" whoever caused it, an icy glare, a cool pronouncement of hate—or a simple statement of fact, "I am angry at you because" (in 25 words or less). Or may I, if need be, turn my anger into energy and shovel the walk, bowl, or play a game of tennis, or clean the house. I pray that God will show me appropriate ways to deal with my anger.

Today I Will Remember

"I am angry because..."

Reflection for the Day

We learn in the Program that we cannot punish anyone without punishing ourselves. The release of my tensions, even justified, in a punishing way leaves behind the dregs of bitterness and pain. This was the monotonous story of my life before I came to the Program. So in my new life, "I'd do well to consider the long-range benefits of simply owning my emotions, naming them and thus releasing them. *Does the voice of God have a chance to be heard over my reproachful shouting?*

Today I Pray

May I avoid name-calling, ego-crushing exchanges. If I am angry, may I try to assign my anger to what someone did instead of what someone is. May I refrain from downgrading, lashing out at character flaws, or mindless abuse. May I count on my Higher Power to show me the way.

Today I Will Remember

To deal with anger appropriately.

Reflection for the Day

When a person says something rash or ugly, we sometimes say they are "forgetting themselves," meaning they're forgetting their best selves in a sudden outburst of uncontrolled fury. If I remember the kind of person I want to be, hopefully I won't "forget myself" and yield to a fit of temper. I'll believe that the positive always defeats the negative: courage overcomes fear; patience overcomes anger and irritability; love overcomes hatred. *Am I always striving for improvement?*

Today I Pray

Today I ask that God, to Whom all things are possible, help me turn negatives into positives—anger into super-energy, fear into a chance to be courageous, hatred into love. May I take time out to remember examples of such positive-from-negative transformations from the whole of my lifetime. Uppermost is God's miracle: my freedom from the slavery of addiction.

Today I Will Remember

Turn negatives into positives.

Reflection for the Day

We are often told in the Program that "more will be revealed." As we are restored to health and become increasingly able to live comfortably in the real world without using chemicals, we begin to see many things in a new light. Many of us have come to realize, for example, that our arch-enemy, anger, comes disguised in many shapes and colors: intolerance, contempt, snobbishness, rigidity, tension, sarcasm, distrust, anxiety, envy, hatred, cynicism, discontent, self-pity, malice, suspicion, jealousy. *Do I let my feelings get the best of me?*

Today I Pray

May I recognize that my anger, like a dancer at a masquerade, wears many forms and many faces. May I strip off its several masks and know it for what it is.

Today I Will Remember

Anger wears a thousand masks.

Reflection for the Day

Do I waste my time and energy wrestling with situations that aren't actually worth a second thought? Like Don Quixote, the bemused hero of Spanish literature, do I imagine windmills as menacing giants, battling them until I am ready to drop from exhaustion? Today, I'll not allow my imagination to build small troubles into big ones. I'll try to see each situation clearly, giving it only the value and attention it deserves. *Have I come to believe, as the second of the Twelve Steps suggests, that a Power greater than myself can restore me to sanity?*

Today I Pray

God, keep my perspective sane. Help me to avoid aggrandizing petty problems, tying too much significance to casual conversations, making a Vesuvius out of an anthill. Keep my fears from swelling out of scale, like shadows on a wall. Restore my values, which became distorted during the days of my chemical involvement.

Today I Will Remember

Sanity is perspective.

Reflection for the Day

When I came to the Program, I found people who knew exactly what I meant when I spoke finally of my fears. They had been where I had been; they *understood*. I've since learned that many of my fears have to do with projection. It's normal, for example, to have a tiny "back-burner" fear that the person I love will leave me. But when the fear takes the precedence over my present and very real relationship with the person I'm afraid of losing, then I'm in trouble. My responsibility to myself includes this: I must not fear things which do not exist. *Am I changing from a fearful person into a fearless person?*

Today I Pray

I ask God's help in waving away my fears—those figments, fantasies, monstrous thoughts, projections of disaster which have no bearing on the present. May I narrow the focus of my imagination and concentrate on the here-and-now, for I tend to see the future through a magnifying glass.

Today I Will Remember

Projected fears, like shadows, are larger than life.

Reflection for the Day

The Twelve Steps teach us that, as faith grows, so does security. The terrifying fear of nothingness begins to subside. As we work the Program, we find that the basic antidote for fear is a spiritual awakening. We lose the fear of making decisions, for we realize that if our choice proves wrong, we can learn from the experience. And should our decision be the right one, we can thank God for giving us the courage and the grace that caused us so to act. *Am I grateful for the courage and grace I receive from my Higher Power?*

Today I Pray

I ask that I be given the power to act, knowing that I have at least a half-chance to make the right decision and that I can learn from a wrong one. For so long, decision-making seemed beyond my capabilities. Now, I can find joy in being able to make choices. Thank you, God, for courage.

Today I Will Remember

Freedom is choosing.

Reflection for the Day

I can banish fear by realizing the truth. Am I afraid to be alone? This fear can be banished by the realization that I am never alone, that God is always with me wherever I am and whatever I do. Am I afraid that I won't have enough money to meet my needs? This fear can be banished by the realization that God is my inexhaustible, unfailing resource, now and always. Today I have the power to change fear into faith. *Can I say with confidence, "I will trust, and will not be afraid..."?*

Today I Pray

That I may fear no evil, for God is with me. That I may learn to turn to my Higher Power when I am afraid. I pray diligently that my faith in God and trust in what He has in store for me is strong enough to banish the fears that undermine my courage.

Today I will Remember

Turn fear into faith.

Reflection for the Day

Before we came to the Program, fear ruled our lives. Tyrannized by our addictions and obsessions, we feared everything and everybody. We feared ourselves and, perhaps most of all, feared fear itself. These days, when I am able to accept the help of my Higher Power, it makes me feel capable of doing anything I am called upon to do. I am overcoming my fears and acquiring a comfortable new confidence. *Can I believe that "courage is fear that has said its prayers..."?*

Today I Pray

God grant that through faith in Him I may overcome my obsessive fears. I have been running scared for so long it has become a habit. God help me to see that I may be purposely clinging to my fears to avoid making decisions, perhaps even to shirk the responsibility of success.

Today I Will Remember

Fear keeps me safe from risk-taking.

Reflection for the Day

"What if..." How often we hear these words from newcomers to the Program. How often, in fact, we tend to say them ourselves. *"What if* I lose my job?" *"What if* my car breaks down?" *"What if* I get sick and can't work?" *"What if* my child gets hooked on drugs?" What if—anything our desperate imaginings can project. Only two small words, yet how heavy-laden they are with dread, fear, and anxiety. The answer to "What if..." is, plainly and simply, "Don't panic." We can only live with our problems as they arise, living one day at a time. *Am I keeping my thoughts positive?*

Today I Pray

May I grow spiritually, without being held back by anxieties. May projected fears not hobble my pursuits or keep me from making the most of today. May I turn out fear by faith. If I will only make a place for God within me, He will remove my fears.

Today I Will Remember

I can only borrow trouble at high interest rates.

Reflection for the Day

If I live just one day at a time, I won't so quickly entertain fears of what *might* happen tomorrow. As long as I'm concentrating on today's activities, there won't be room in my mind for worrying. I'll try to fill every minute of this day with something good—seen, heard, accomplished. Then, when the day is ended, I'll be able to look back on it with satisfaction, serenity, and gratitude. *Do I sometimes cherish bad feelings so that I can feel sorry for myself?*

Today I Pray

That I will get out of the self-pity act and live for today. May I notice the good things from dawn to nightfall, learn to talk about them and thank God for them. May I catch myself if I seem to be relishing my moans and complaints more often than appreciating the goodness of my life.

Today I Will Remember

Today is good.

Reflection for the Day

We're taught in the Program and the Twelve Steps that the chief activator of our defects has been self-centered fear—mainly fear that we would lose something we already possessed or that we would fail to get something we demanded. Living on the basis of unsatisfied demands, we obviously were in a state of continual disturbance and frustration. Therefore, we are taught, no peace will be ours unless we find a means of producing these demands. *Have I become entirely ready to have God remove all my defects of character?*

Today I Pray

May I make no unrealistic demands on life, which, because of their grandiosity, cannot be met. May I place no excessive demands on others which, when they are not fulfilled, leave me disappointed and let down.

Today I Will Remember

The set-up for a let-down.

Reflection for the Day

Just for today, I'll not be afraid of anything. If my mind is clouded with nameless fears, I'll track them down and expose their unreality. I'll remind myself that God is in charge of me and my life, and that all I have to do is accept His protection and guidance. What happened yesterday need not trouble me today. *Do I accept the fact that it's in my power to make today a good one just by the way I think about it and what I do about it?*

Today I Pray

May I make today a good day. May I know that it is up to me to assign to it qualities of goodness, through a positive attitude toward what the present is providing. May I be untroubled by vestiges of yesterday. Please, God, remain close to me all through this day.

Today I Will Remember

To make it good.

Reflection for the Day

Now that we're free and no longer chemically dependent, we have so much more control over our thinking. More than anything, we're able to alter our attitudes. Some members of Alcoholics Anonymous, in fact, choose to think of the letters AA as an abbreviation for "Altered Attitudes." In the bad old days, I almost always responded to any optimistic or positive statement with "Yes, but..." Today, in contrast, I'm learning to eliminate that negative phrase from my vocabulary. *Am I working to change my attitude? Am I determined to "accentuate the positive..."?*

Today I Pray

May I find that healing and strength which God provides to those who stay near Him. May I keep to the spiritual guidelines of the Program, considering the Steps, taking the Steps—one by one—then practicing them again and again. In this is my salvation.

Today I Will Remember

To practice at least one Step.

Reflection for the Day

Why don't I spend part of today thinking about my assets, rather than my liabilities? Why not think about victories, instead of defeats—about the ways in which I am gentle and kind? It's always been my tendency to fall into a sort of cynical self-hypnosis, putting derogatory labels on practically everything I've done, said, or felt. Just for today, I'll spend a quiet half hour trying to gain a more positive perspective on my life. *Do I have the courage to change the things I can?*

Today I Pray

Through quietness and a reassessment of myself, may I develop a more positive attitude. If I am a child of God, created in God's image, there must be goodness in me. I will think about that goodness, and the ways it manifests itself. I will stop putting myself down, even in my secret thoughts. I will respect what is God's. I will respect myself.

Today I Will Remember

Self-respect is respect for God.

Reflection for the Day

I've begun to understand myself better since I've come to the Program. One of the most important things I've learned is that *opinions* aren't *facts*. Just because I feel that a thing is so doesn't necessarily *make* it so. "Men are not worried by things," wrote the Greek philosopher Epictetus, "but by their ideas about things. When we meet with difficulties, become anxious or troubled, let us not blame others, but rather ourselves. That is: our ideas about things." *Do I believe that I can never entirely lose what I have learned during my recovery?*

Today I Pray

May I learn to sort out realities from my ideas about those realities. May I understand that situations, things—even people—take on the colors and dimensions of my attitudes about them.

Today I Will Remember

To sort the real from the unreal.

Reflection for the Day

We may not know any specifics about the activities of today; we may not know whether we'll be alone or with others. We may feel the day contains too much time—or not enough. We may be facing tasks we're eager to complete, or tasks we've been resisting. Though the details of each person's day differ, each person's day does hold one similarity: each of us has the opportunity to choose to think positive thoughts. The choice depends less on our outside activities than on our inner commitment. *Can I accept that I alone have the power to control my attitude?*

Today I Pray

May I keep the fire of inner commitment alive through this whole, glorious day, whether my activities are a succession of workaday tasks or free-form and creative. May I choose to make this a good day for me, and for those around me.

Today I Will Remember

Keep the commitment.

Reflection for the Day

Before I became sober in the Program, I blamed all my problems on other people, or on places and things. Now I'm learning to look squarely at each difficulty, not seeking whom to "blame," but to discover how my attitude helped create my problem or aggravate it. I must also learn to face the consequences of my own actions and words, and to correct myself when I'm wrong. *Do I practice the Tenth Step by continuing to take personal inventory? When I am wrong, do I promptly admit it?*

Today I Pray

May I know the blessed relief and unburdening that come when I admit I have done something wrong. May I learn—perhaps for the first time in my entire life—to take responsibility for my own actions and to face the consequences. May I learn again how to match actions with consequences.

Today I Will Remember

To take responsibility for my own actions.

Reflection for the Day

There is no advantage, no profits, and certainly no growth when I deceive myself merely to escape the consequences of my own mistakes. When I realize this, I know I'll be making progress. "We must be true inside, true to ourselves, before we can know a truth that is outside us," wrote Thomas Merton in *No Man Is an Island*. "But we make ourselves true inside by manifesting the truth as we see it." *Am I true to myself?*

Today I Pray

May I count on my Higher Power to help me carry out the truth as I see it. May I never duck a consequence again. Consequence-ducking became a parlor game for chemically addictive persons like me, until we lost all sense of relationship between action and outcome. Now that I am healing, please God, restore my balance.

Today I Will Remember

Match the act with the consequence.

Reflection for the Day

It's time for me to realize that my attitude—toward the life I'm living and the people in it—can have a tangible, measurable, and profound effect on what happens to me day by day. If I expect good, then good will surely come to me. And if I try each day to base my attitude and point of view on a sound spiritual foundation, I know it will change all the circumstances of my life for the better, too. *Do I accept the fact that I have been given only a daily reprieve that is contingent on the maintenance of my spiritual condition?*

Today I Pray

Since my illness was spiritual—as well as physical and emotional—may I mend spiritually through daily communion with God. May I find a corner of quiet within me where I can spend a few moments with God. May God's will be known to me. May I worship God from that inner temple that is in myself.

Today I Will Remember

To spend a quiet moment with God.

Reflection for the Day

Merely to change my behavior, and what I say and do, doesn't prove there's been a change in my actual inner attitude. I'm deceiving myself if I believe I can somehow completely disguise my true feelings. They'll somehow come through, prolonging the difficulties in my relationships with others. I have to avoid half-measures in getting rid of the troublesome emotions I've been trying to hide. *Have I taken an honest inventory of myself?*

Today I Pray

May I know that feelings will come out somehow—sometimes barely disguised as behavior that I cannot always understand. But that perhaps is more acceptable to me than the root emotion that caused it. May I be completely and vigilantly honest with myself. May I be given the insight that comes through depending upon a Higher Power.

Today I Will Remember

Feelings can come out "sideways."

Reflection for the Day

We learn in the Program and its Twelve Steps that, as we grow spiritually, we find that our old attitudes toward our instinctual drives need to undergo drastic revisions. Our demands for emotional security and wealth, for personal prestige and power, all have to be tempered and redirected. We learn that the full satisfaction of these demands cannot be the sole end and aim of our lives. But when we're willing to place spiritual growth first—then and only then do we have a real chance to grow in healthy awareness and mature love. *Am I willing to place spiritual growth first?*

Today I Pray

May my development as a spiritual person temper my habitual hankerings for material security. May I understand that the only real security in life is spiritual. If I have faith in my Higher Power, these revisions in my attitudes will follow. May I grow first in spiritual awareness.

Today I Will Remember

Value the life of the spirit.

Reflection for the Day

In a letter to a friend, AA's co-founder Bill W. once wrote: "Nothing can be more demoralizing than a clinging and abject dependence upon another human being. This often amounts to the demand for a degree of protection and love that no one could possibly satisfy. So our hoped-for protectors finally flee, and once more we are left alone—either to grow up or to disintegrate." We discover, in the Program, that the best possible source of emotional stability is our Higher Power. We find that dependence upon His perfect justice, forgiveness, and love is healthy, and that it works where nothing else will. *Do I depend on my Higher Power?*

Today I Pray

May I realize that I am a dependent person. I have depended upon chemicals to alter my moods and attitudes. I have also developed parasitic attachments for others. May I stop making unrealistic emotional demands on others, which only serve to choke off mature human relationships and to leave me bewildered and let down. Only God can provide the kind of whole-hearted love which I, as a dependent person, seem to need. May I depend first upon God.

Today I Will Remember

God offers perfect love.

Reflection for the Day

Since I came to the Program, I've begun to recognize my previous inability to form a true partnership with another person. It seems that my egomania created two disasterous pitfalls. Either I insisted upon dominating the people I knew, or I depended on them far too much. My friends in the Program have taught me that my dependence meant demand—a demand for the possession and control of the people and the conditions surrounding me. *Do I still try to find emotional security either by dominating or being dependent on others?*

Today I Pray

May I turn first to God to satisfy my love-hunger, knowing that all He asks from me is my faith in Him. May I no longer cast emotional nets over those I love, either by dominating them or being excessively dependent upon them—which is just another form of domination. May I give others the room they need to be themselves. May God show me the way to mature human relationships.

Today I Will Remember

To have faith in God's love.

Reflection for the Day

If we examine every disturbance we have, great or small, we'll find at the root of it some unhealthy dependency and its consequent unhealthy demand. So let us, with God's help, continually surrender these crippling liabilities. Then we can be set free to live and love. We may then be able to Twelfth Step ourselves, as well as others, into emotional sobriety. *Do I try to carry the message of the Program?*

Today I Pray

May I first get my emotional and spiritual house in order before I seek to carry out serious commitments in human relationships. May I look long and thoroughly at "dependency"—upon alcohol or other drugs or upon other human beings—and recognize it as the source of my unrest. May I transfer my dependency to God, as I understand Him.

Today I Will Remember

I am God-dependent.

Reflection for the Day

All my life, I looked to others for comfort, security, and all the other things that add up to what I now call serenity. But I've come to realize that I was always looking in the wrong place. The source of serenity is not outside, but within myself. The kingdom is within me, and I already have the key. All I have to do is to be willing to use it. *Am I using the tools of the Program on a daily basis? Am I willing?*

Today I Pray

God gave me the courage to seek out the kingdom inside myself, to find that well-spring within me which has its source in the neverending, life-giving receiver of God. May my soul be restored there. May I find the serenity I seek.

Today I Will Remember

To seek the inner kingdom.

Reflection for the Day

One thing that keeps me on the right track today is a feeling of loyalty to other members of the Program, no matter where they may be. We depend on each other. I know, for example, that I'd be letting them down if I ever took a drink. When I came into the Program, I found a group of people who were not only helping each other to stay sober, but who were loyal to each other by staying sober themselves. *Am I loyal to my group and to my friends in the Program?*

Today I Pray

I thank God for the loyalty and fellowship of the group and for the mutuality of commitment that binds us together. May I give to the group in the same proportion that I take from it. Having been a taker during so many of my years, my giving used to be no more than a commodity, for which I expected to be paid in approval or love or favors. May I learn the joy of pure giving, with no strings attached, no expectation of reward.

Today I Will Remember

A perfect gift asks nothing in return.

Reflection for the Day

There have been days during my recovery when just about everything seemed bleak and even hopeless. I allowed myself to become depressed and angry. I see now that it doesn't matter what I think, and it doesn't matter how I feel. It's what I do that counts. So when I become anxious or upset, I try to get into action by going to meetings, participating, and working with others in the Program. *If God seems far away, who moved?*

Today I Pray

May I not be immobilized by sadness or anger to the point of despair. May I look for the roots of despair in my tangle of emotions, sort out the tangle, pull out the culprit feelings, acknowledge that they belong to me. Only then can I get into gear, take action, begin to accomplish. May I learn to make use of the energy generated by anger to strengthen my will and achieve my goals.

Today I Will Remember

To sort out my feelings.

Reflection for the Day

The Program teaches us that we are bodily and mentally different from our fellows. We are reminded that the great obsession of every abnormal drinker—and every one of us who is otherwise addictive—is to prove that somehow, someday, we will be able to control our drinking, eating, or gambling. The persistence of this illusion is astonishing, we are told, and many pursue it to the gates of insanity or death. *Have I conceded to my innermost self that, for me, "One is too many and a thousand not enough..."?*

Today I Pray

May I have no illusions about someday becoming a moderate drinker or drug-user after being an obsessive one. May I muffle any small voice of destructive pride which lies to me, telling me that I can now go back to my former use and control it. This is a Program of no return, and I thank God for it.

Today I Will Remember

My goal must be lifelong abstinence—a day at a time.

Reflection for the Day

"Lead us not into temptation," we pray, for we know with certainty that temptation lurks around the corner. Temptation is cunning, baffling, powerful—and patient; we never know when it will catch us with our guard down. Temptation could come in the siren song of a four-color advertisement, the fragment of a help-remembered song or, more obviously, in the direct urgings of another person. We must remain forever vigilant, remembering that the first drink gets us drunk, that the first obsessive bite will likely trigger an overeating orgy, that the first roll of the dice could well destroy our lives. *Am I aware of my number one priority?*

Today I Pray

God, lead me out of temptation—whether it is the jolly-alcoholic abandon of my peers at a special-occasion celebration, the pressure from my friends to "get in the spirit" of a party, the familiar aura of an apartment where joints are passed around, the sound of rattling dice, the smell of a bakery. May I know the limits of my resistance and stay well within them. May my surrender to the will of God give a whole new meaning to that old phrase, "Get in the spirit."

Today I Will Remember

Get in the spirit.

Reflection for the Day

In the old days, we often had such devastating experiences that we fervently swore, "Never again." We were absolutely sincere in those moments of desperation. Yet, despite our intentions, the outcome was inevitably the same. Eventually, the memory of our suffering faded, as did the memory of our "pledge." So we did it again, ending up in even worse shape than when we had last "sworn off." Forever turned out to be only a week, or a day, or less. In the Program, we learn that we need only be concerned about today, this particular 24-hour period. *Do I live my life just 24 hours at a time?*

Today I Pray

May the long-term requirements of such phrases as "never again," "not on your life," "forever," "I'll never take another..." not weaken my resolve. "Forever," when it is broken down into single days—or even just parts of days—does not seem so impossibly long. May I awake each day with my goal set realistically at just 24 hours.

Today I Will Remember

Twenty-four hours at a time.

Reflection for the Day

I know today that "stopping in for a drink" will never again be—for me—simply killing a few minutes and leaving a buck on a bar. In exchange for the first drink, what I'd pluck down now would be my bank account, my family, our home, our car, my job, my sanity, and probably my life. It's too big a price, and too great a risk. *Do you remember your last drunk?*

Today I Pray

May I be strong in the knowledge that God's spirit is with me at all times. May I learn to feel that spiritual presence. May I know that nothing is hidden from God. Unlike the world, which approves or disapproves of my outward behavior, God sees all that I do, think, or feel. If I seek to do God's will, I can always count on reward for me—peace of mind.

Today I Will Remember

God knows all.

Reflection for the Day

The longer I'm in the Program, the more important becomes the slogan "First Things First." I used to believe that my family came first, that my home life came first, that my job came first. But I know today, in the depths of my heart, that if I can't stay sober, I'll have nothing. "First Things First," to me, means that everything in my life depends on my sobriety. *Am I grateful to be sober today?*

Today I Pray

May my first priority, the topmost item on my list of concerns, be my sobriety—maintaining it, learning to live comfortably with it, sharing the tools by which I maintain it. When other things crowd into my life and I am caught up in the busyness of living, may I still preserve that first-of-all goal—remaining free of chemicals.

Today I Will Remember

First Things First.

Reflection for the Day

The Program teaches us that we have an incurable illness. We always get worse, never better. But we're fortunate in that our incurable illness can be arrested, so long as we don't take the first drink, one day at a time. High-toned academic research and ivory-tower studies to the contrary, we know from experience that we can no more control our drinking than we can control the ocean tides. *Do I have any doubt that I am powerless over alcohol?*

Today I Pray

May I never fall prey to any short-term research results which tell me that alcoholism can be cured, that I would be safe to begin drinking again, supposedly, in a responsible manner. My experience—and the experience of those in the Program—will outshout such theories. May I know that my disease is arrestable, but not curable. May I know that if I took up my active addiction again, I would begin where I left off—closer than ever to possible death or insanity.

Today I Will Remember

Be wary of new theories.

Reflection for the Day

Once in a great while, I find myself thinking that perhaps things weren't quite so bad as they seemed to be. At such moments, I force myself to realize that my *illness* is talking to me, trying to tempt me into denying that I am, in fact, afflicted with an illness. One of the key action steps of the Program is that we give our illness to God as we understand Him, accepting our powerlessness in the face of His greater Power. *Do I believe that the grace of God can do for me what I could never do for myself?*

Today I Pray

May I know that much of our lives depends on faith. For we cannot know the limits of space and time—or explain the mysteries of life and death. But when we see God working through us—and through others who have found new life in the Program—it is all the evidence we need to know that God exists.

Today I Will Remember

The Big Wheel runs by faith.

Reflection for the Day

The Program teaches us, through the experience, strength, and hope of its fellowship, that the worst situation imaginable does not warrant a return to our addiction. No matter how bad a particular situation or set of circumstances, the return to our old ways for even a minute will assuredly make it worse. *Am I grateful for the sharing and caring of the Program?*

Today I Pray

May I insist that no stone can be heavy enough to drag me back down into the pool of my addiction. No burden, no disappointment, no blow to pride or loss of human love is worth the price of returning to my old way of life. When I harbor thoughts that life is "too much" for me, that no one should be expected to "take so much and still remain sane" or that I am "the fall guy," let me listen for the tone of my complaints and remember that I have heard that whine before—before I concluded that I was powerless over the chemical and gave my will over to the Will of God. Such wailing sets me up for getting high again. May God keep my ears alert to the tone of my own complaining.

Today I Will Remember

Hear my own complaints.

Reflection for the Day

All of us are faced with the troubles and problems of daily living, whether we've been in the Program two days or twenty years. We'd sometimes like to believe we could take care of all our problems *right now,* but it rarely works that way. If we remember the slogan "Easy Does It" when we are ready to panic, we may come to know that the very best way to handle all things is "Easy." We put one foot in front of the other, doing the best we are capable of doing. We say "Easy Does It," and we *do* it. *Are the Program's slogans growing with me as I grow with the Program?*

Today I Pray

May even the words "Easy Does It" serve to slow me down in my headlong rush to accomplish too much too fast. May just that word "Easy" be enough to make me ease up on the accelerator which plunges me into new situations without enough forethought, ease off on the number of hours spent in material pursuits. May I hark to the adage that Rome wasn't built in a single day. Neither can I build solutions to my problems all at once.

Today I Will Remember

Easy Does It.

Reflection for the Day

If a chemically dependent person wants to live successfully in society, he or she must replace the power of chemicals over his/her life with the power of something else—preferably positive, at least neutral, but not negative. That is why we say to the agnostic newcomer: If you can't believe in God, find a positive power that is as great as the power of your addiction, and give it the power and dependence you gave to your addiction. In the Program, the agnostic is left free to find his or her Higher Power, and can use the principles of the Program and the therapy of the meetings to aid in rebuilding his/her life. *Do I go out of my way to work with newcomers?*

Today I Pray

May the Power of the Program work its miracles equally for those who believe in the personal God or in a Universal spirit or in the strength of the group itself, or for those who define their Higher Power in their own terms, religious or not. If newcomers are disturbed by the religiosity of the Program, may I welcome them on their own spiritual terms. May I recognize that we are all spiritual beings.

Today I Will Remember

To each his own spirituality.

Reflection for the Day

I know today that getting active means trying to live the suggested Steps of the Program to the best of my ability. It means striving for some degree of honesty, first with myself, then with others. It means activity directed inward, to enable me to see myself and my relationship with my Higher Power more clearly. As I get active, outside and inside myself, so shall I grow in the Program. *Do I let others do all the work at meetings? Do I carry my share?*

Today I Pray

May I realize that "letting go and letting God" does not mean that I do not have to put any effort into the Program. It is up to me to work the Twelve Steps, to learn what may be an entirely new thing with me—honesty. May I differentiate between activity for activity's sake—busy-work to keep me from thinking—and the thoughtful activity which helps me to grow.

Today I Will Remember

"Letting God" means letting God show us how.

Reflection for the Day

Storing up grievances is not only a waste of time, but a waste of life that could be lived to greater satisfaction. If I keep a ledger of "oppressions and indignities," I'm only restoring them to painful reality.

" 'The horror of that moment,' the King said, 'I shall never, never forget.'
" 'You will though, if you don't make a memorandum of it.' "

(Lewis Carroll, *Through The Looking Glass*)

Am I keeping a secret storehouse for the wreckage of my past?

Today I Pray

God keep me from harboring the sludge for the past—grievances, annoyances, grudges, oppressions, wrongs, injustices, put-downs, slights, hurts. They will nag at me and consume my time in rehashing what I "might have said" or done until I face each one, name the emotion it produces in me, settle it as best I can—and forget it. May I empty my storehouse of old grievances.

Today I Will Remember

Don't rattle old bones.

Reflection for the Day

We must think deeply of all those sick persons still to come to the Program. As they try to make their return to faith and to life, we want them to find everything in the Program that we have found, yet more, if that be possible. No care, no vigilance, no effort to preserve the Program's constant effectiveness and spiritual strength will ever be too great to hold us in full readiness for the day of their homecoming. *How well do I respect the Traditions of the Program?*

Today I Pray

God, help me to carry out my part in making the group a lifeline for those who are still suffering from addictions, in maintaining the Steps and the Traditions which have made it work for me for those who are still to come. May the Program be a "homecoming" for those of us who share the disease of addiction. May we find common solutions to the common problems which that disease breeds.

Today I Will Remember

To do my part.

Reflection for the Day

What is the definition of humility? "Absolute humility," said AA co-founder Bill W., "would consist of a state of complete freedom from myself, freedom from all the claims that my defects of character now lay so heavily upon me. Perfect humility would be a full willingness, in all times and places, to find and to do the will of God." *Am I striving for humility?*

Today I Pray

May God expand my interpretation of humility beyond abject subservience or awe at the greatness of others. May humility also mean freedom from myself, a freedom which can come only through turning my being over to God's will. May I sense the omnipotence of God, which is simultaneously humbling and exhilarating. May I be willing to carry out God's will.

Today I Will Remember

Humility is freedom.

Reflection for the Day

"When I meditate upon such a vision," Bill W. continued, "I need not be dismayed because I shall never attain it, nor need I swell with presumption that one of these days its virtues shall all be mine. I only need to dwell on the vision itself, letting it grow and ever more fill my heart...Then I get a sane and healthy idea of where I stand on the highway to humility. I see that my journey towards God has scarcely begun. As I thus get down to my right size and stature, my self-concern and importance become amusing." *Do I take myself too seriously?*

Today I Pray

May the grandiosity which is a symptom of my chemical addiction be brought back into proportion by the simple comparison of my powerlessness with the power of God. May I think of the meaning of Higher Power as it relates to my human frailty. May it bring my ego back down to scale and help me shed my defenses of pomp or bluster or secret ideas of self-importance.

Today I Will Remember

God is great. I am small.

Reflection for the Day

My illness is unlike most other illnesses in that *denial* that I am sick is a primary symptom that I am sick. Like such other incurable illnesses as diabetes and arthritis, however, my illness is characterized by relapses. In the Program, we call such relapses "slips." The one thing I know for certain is that I alone can cause myself to slip. *Will I remember at all times that the thought precedes the action? Will I try to avoid "stinking thinking"?*

Today I Pray

May God give me the power to resist temptations. May the responsibility for giving in, for having a "slip," be on my shoulders and mine only. May I see *beforehand* if I am setting myself up for a slip by blame-shifting, shirking my responsibility to myself, becoming the world's poor puppet once again. My return to those old attitudes can be as much of a slip as the act of losing my sobriety.

Today I Will Remember

Nobody's slip-proof.

Reflection for the Day

If we don't want to slip, we'll avoid slippery places. For the alcoholic, that means avoiding old drinking haunts; for the overeater, that means by-passing a once-favorite pastry shop; for the gambler, that means shunning poker parties and racetracks. For me, certain emotional situations can also be slippery places; so can indulgence of old ideas such as a well-nourished resentment that is allowed to build to explosive proportions. *Do I carry the principles of the Program with me wherever I go?*

Today I Pray

May I learn not to test myself too harshly by "asking for it," by stopping in at the bar or the bakery or the track. Such "testing" can be dangerous, especially if I am egged on, not only by a thirst or an appetite or a craving for the old object of my addictions, but by others still caught in addiction whose moral responsibility has been reduced to zero.

Today I Will Remember

Avoid slippery places.

Reflection for the Day

What causes slips? What happens to a person who apparently seems to understand and live the way of the Program, yet decides to go out again? What can I do to keep this from happening to me? Is there any consistency among those who slip, any common denominators that seem to apply? We can each draw our own conclusions, but we learn in the Program that certain inactions will all but guarantee an eventual slip. *When a person who has slipped is fortunate enough to return to the Program, do I listen carefully to what he or she says about the slip?*

Today I Pray

May my Higher Power—if I listen—show me if I am setting myself up to get high again. May I glean from the experiences of others that the reasons for such a lapse of resolve or such an accident of will most often stem from what I have not done rather than from what I have done. May I "keep coming back" to meetings.

Today I Will Remember

Keep coming back.

Reflection for the Day

In almost every instance, the returned slipper says, "I stopped going to meetings," or "I got fed up with the same old stories and the same old faces," or "My outside commitments were such that I had to cut down on meetings," or "I felt I'd received the optimum benefits from the meetings, so I sought further help from more meaningful activities." In short, they simply stopped going to meetings. A saying I've heard in the Program hits the nail on the head: "Them which stops going to meetings are not present at meetings to hear about what happens to them that stops going to meetings." *Am I going to enough meetings for me?*

Today I Pray

God keep me on the track of the Program. May I never be too tired, too busy, too complacent, too bored to go to meetings. Almost always those complaints are reversed at a meeting if I will just get myself there. My weariness dissipates in serenity. My busyness is reduced to its rightful proportion. My complacency gives way to vigilance again. And how can I be bored in a place where there is so much fellowship and joy?

Today I Will Remember

Attend the meetings.

Reflection for the Day

Another common denominator among those who slip is failure to use the tools of the Program—the Twelve Steps. The comments heard most often are, "I never did work the Steps," "I never got past the First Step," "I worked the steps too slow," or "too fast" or "too soon." What it boils down to, is that these people considered the Steps, but didn't conscientiously and sincerely apply the Steps to their lives. *Am I learning how to protect myself and help others?*

Today I Pray

May I be a doer of the Steps and not a hearer only. May I see some of the common mis-Steps which lead to a fall: being too proud to admit Step One; being too tied to everyday earth to feel the presence of a Higher Power; being overwhelmed by the thought of preparing Step Four, a complete moral inventory; being too reticent to share that inventory. Please God, guide me as I work the Twelve Steps.

Today I Will Remember

To watch my Steps.

Reflection for the Day

Still another common thread we invariably see among slippers is that many of them felt dissatisfaction with today. "I forgot we live one day at a time," or "I began to anticipate the future," or "I began to plan *results,* not just plan." They seemed to forget that all we have is Now. Life continued to get better for them and, as many of us do, they forgot how bad it had been. They began to think, instead, of how dissatisfying it was compared to what it *could be. Do I compare today with yesterday, realizing, by that contrast, what great benefits and blessings I have today?*

Today I Pray

If I am discouraged with today, may I remember the sorrows and hassles of yesterday. If I am impatient for the future, let me appreciate today and how much better it is than the life I left behind. May I never forget the principle of "one day at a time..."

Today I Will Remember

The craziness of yesterday.

Reflection for the Day

What do we say to a person who has slipped, or one who calls for help? We can carry the message, if they're willing to listen; we can share our experience, strength, and hope. Perhaps the most important thing we can do, however, is to tell the person that we love him or her, that we're truly happy he or she is back, and that we want to help all we can. And we must mean it. *Can I still "go to school" and continue to learn from the mistakes and adversities of others?*

Today I Pray

May I always have enough love to welcome back to the group someone who has slipped. May I listen to that person's story-of-woe, humbly. For there, but for my Higher Power, go I. May I learn from others' mistakes and pray that I will not re-enact them.

Today I Will Remember

Sobriety is never fail-safe.

Reflection for the Day

Our spiritual and emotional growth in the Program doesn't depend so deeply upon success as it does upon our failures and setbacks. If we bear this in mind, a relapse can have the effect of kicking us upstairs, instead of down. We in the Program have had no better teacher than Old Man Adversity, except in those cases where we refuse to let him teach us. *Do I try to remain always teachable?*

Today I Pray

May I respect the total Program, with its unending possibilities for spiritual and emotional growth, so that I can view a relapse as a learning experience, not "the end of the world." May relapse for any one of our fellowship serve to teach not only the person who has slipped, but all of us. May it strengthen our shared resolve.

Today I Will Remember

If you slip, get up.

Reflection for the Day

Time after time, we learn in the Program, new-comers try to keep to themselves "shoddy facts" about their lives. Trying to avoid the humbling experience of the Fifth Step, they turn to a seemingly easier and softer way. Almost invariably, they slip. Having persevered with the rest of the Program, they then wonder why they fell. The probable reason is that they never completed their housecleaning. They took inventory all right, but hung on to some of the worst items in stock. *Have I admitted to God, to myself, and to another human being the exact nature of my wrongs?*

Today I Pray

That I may include all of the sleaziness of my past, my cruelties and my dishonesties, in a complete moral inventory of myself. May I hold back nothing out of shame or pride, for the "exact nature" of my wrongs means just that—a thorough and exact recounting of past mistakes and character flaws. We have been provided with an appropriate "dumping-ground." May I use it as it was intended. May all my throw-aways, the trash and outgrown costumes of the past, be foundation "fill" on which to build a new life.

Today I Will Remember

Trash can be a foundation for treasures.

Reflection for the Day

Faith is more than our greatest gift; sharing it with others is our greatest responsibility. May we of the Program continually seek the wisdom and the willingness by which we may well fulfill the immense trust which the Giver of all perfect gifts has placed in our hands. *If you pray, why worry? If you worry, why pray?*

Today I Pray

Our God is a mighty fortress, a bulwark who never fails us. May we give praise for our deliverance and for our protection. God gives us the gift of faith to share. May we pass it along to others as best we know how and in the loving spirit in which it was given to us.

Today I Will Remember

God will not fail us.

APRIL 10

Reflection for the Day

Change is the characteristic of all growth. From drinking to sobriety, from dishonesty to honesty, from conflict to serenity, from childish dependence to adult responsibility—all this and infinitely more represent change for the better. Only God is unchanging; only He has all the truth there is. *Do I accept the belief that lack of power was my dilemma? Have I found a power by which I can live—a Power greater than myself?*

Today I Pray

I pray that the Program will be, for me, an outline for change—for changing me. These days of transition from active addiction to sobriety, from powerlessness to power through God, may be rocky, as change can be. May my restlessness be stilled by the unchanging nature of God, in whom I place my trust. Only God is whole and perfect and predictable.

Today I Will Remember

I can count on my Higher Power.

Reflection for the Day

I came; I came to; I came to believe. The Program has enabled me to learn that deep down in every man, woman, and child is the fundamental idea of a God. It may be obscured by pomp, by calamity, by worship of other things, but in some form or other it is there. For faith in a Power greater than ourselves and miraculous demonstrations of the Power in human lives are facts as old as man himself. *How well do I share my free gifts?*

Today I Pray

I pray that I may continue to look for—and find—the Godliness that is in me and in every other person, no matter how it is obscured. May I be aware that the consciousness of a Higher Power has been present in man since he was first given the power to reason, no matter what name he gave to it or how he sought to reach it. May my own faith in a Higher Power be reinforced by the experience of all mankind—and by the working of God's gracious miracles in my own life.

Today I Will Remember

God is in us all.

Reflection for the Day

If we attempt to understand rather than to be understood, we can more quickly assure a newcomer that we have no desire to convince anyone that there is only one way by which faith can be acquired. All of us, whatever our race, creed, color, or ethnic heritage, are the children of a living Creator, with whom we may form a relationship upon simple and understandable terms—as soon as we are willing and honest enough to try. *Do I know the difference between sympathy and empathy? Can I put myself in the newcomer's shoes?*

Today I Pray

May I try to love all humanity as children of a living God. May I respect the different ways through which they find and worship Him. May I never be so rigid as to discount another's path to God or so insensitive that I use the fellowship of the group as a preaching ground to extol my religious beliefs as the only way. I can only know what works for me.

Today I Will Remember

We are all children of God.

Reflection for the Day

Any number of addicted people are bedeviled by the dire conviction that if they ever go near the Program—whether by attending meetings or talking one-to-one with a member—they'll be pressured to conform to some particular brand of faith or religion. They don't realize that faith is never an imperative for membership in the Program; that freedom from addiction can be achieved with an easily acceptable minimum of it; and that our concepts of a Higher Power and God—as we understand him—afford everyone a nearly unlimited choice of spiritual belief and action. *Am I receiving strength by sharing with newcomers?*

Today I Pray

May I never frighten newcomers or keep away those who are considering coming to the Program by imposing on them my particular, personal ideas about a Higher Power. May each discover his or her own spiritual identity. May all find within themselves a link with some great universal Being or Spirit whose power is greater than theirs individually. May I grow, both in tolerance and in spirituality, every day.

Today I Will Remember

I will reach, not preach.

Reflection for the Day

Every man and woman who has joined the Program and intends to stick around has, without realizing it, made a beginning on Step Three. Isn't it true that, in all matters related to their addictions, each of them has decided to turn his or her life over to the care, protection, and guidance of the Program? So already a willingness has been achieved to cast out one's own will and one's own ideas about the addiction in favor of those suggested by the Program. If this isn't turning one's will and life over to a new-found "Providence," then what is it? *Have I had a spiritual awakening as the result of the Steps?*

Today I Pray

For myself, I pray for a God-centered life. I thank God often for the spiritual awakening I have felt since I turned my life over to Him. May the words "spiritual awakening" be a clue to others that there is a free fund of spiritual power within each person. It must only be discovered.

Today I Will Remember

I will try to be God-centered.

Reflection for the Day

Rare are the practicing alcoholics who have any idea how irrational they are, or, seeing their irrationality, can bear to face it. One reason is that they are abetted in their blindness by a world which doesn't yet understand the difference between sane drinking and alcoholism. The dictionary defines sanity as "soundness of mind." Yet no alcoholic, soberly analyzing his or her destructive behavior, can truly claim soundness of mind. *Have I come to believe, as the Second Step suggests, that a Power greater than myself can restore me to sanity?*

Today I Pray

May I see that my own behavior as a practicing alcoholic, a drug-user, or a compulsive overeater, could be described as "insane." For those still actively addicted, admitting to "insane" behavior is well-nigh impossible. I pray that I may continue to abhor the *insanities* and *inanities* of my addictive days. May others like me recognize their problems of addiction, find help in treatment and in the Program, and come to believe that a Higher Power can restore them to sanity.

Today I Will Remember

He restoreth my soul.

Reflection for the Day

I once heard it said that "the mind is the slayer of the real." Looking back at the insanity of those days when I was actively addicted, I know precisely what that phrase means. One of the Program's important fringe benefits for me today is an increasing awareness of the world around me, so I can see and enjoy reality. This alone helps diminish the difficulties I so often magnify, creating my own misery in the process. *Am I acquiring the sense of reality which is absolutely essential to serenity?*

Today I Pray

May I be revived by a sharpened sense of reality, excited to see—for the first time since the blur of my worst moments—the wonders and opportunities in my world. Emerging from the don't-care haze of addiction, I see objects and faces coming into focus again, colors brightening. May I take delight in this new-found brightness.

Today I Will Remember

To focus on my realities.

Reflection for the Day

The Program teaches me to remain on guard against impatience, lapses into self-pity, and resentments of the words and deeds of others. Though I must mever forget what it used to be like, neither should I permit myself to take tormenting excursions into the past—merely for the sake of self-indulgent morbidity. Now that I'm alert to the danger signals, I know I'm improving day by day. *If a crisis arises, or any problem baffles me, do I hold it up to the light of the Serenity Prayer?*

Today I Pray

I pray for perspective as I review the past. May I curb my impulse to upstage and outdo the members of my group by regaling them with the horrors of my addiction. May I no longer use the past to document my self-pity or submerge myself in guilt. May memories of those miserable earlier days serve me only as sentinels, guarding against hazardous situations or unhealthy sets of mind.

Today I Will Remember

I cannot change the past.

Reflection for the Day

We in the Program know full well the futility of trying to overcome our addictions by will power alone. At the same time, we do know that it takes great willingness to adopt the Program's Twelve Steps as a way of life that can restore us to sanity. No matter how severe our addictions, we discover with relief that choices can still be made. For example, we can choose to admit that we're personally powerless over chemical dependency; that dependence upon a Higher Power is a necessity, even if this be simply dependence upon our group in the Program. *Have I chosen to try for a life of honesty and humility, of selfless service to my fellows and to God as I understand Him?*

Today I Pray

God grant me the wisdom to know the difference between "will power" (which has failed me before) and "willingness" to seek help for my dependency, through God and through others who are also recovering. May I know that there are choices open to me as there are to my fellow sufferers in the foggiest stages of addiction. May I choose the kind of life God wants for me.

Today I Will Remember

Willingness, more than will power, is the key to recovery.

Reflection for the Day

As we continue to make these vital choices and so move toward these high aspirations, our sanity returns and the compulsion of our former addictions vanishes. We learn, in the words of Plutarch, that, "A pleasant and happy life does not come from external things. Man draws from within himself, as from a spring, pleasure and joy." *Am I learning to "travel first class" inside?*

Today I Pray

The grace of God has showed me how to be happy again. May the wisdom of God teach me that the source of that happiness is within me, in my new values, my new sense of self-worth, my new and open communication with my Higher Power.

Today I Will Remember

Happiness comes from within.

Reflection for the Day

"If a person continues to see only giants," wrote Anais Nin, "it means he is still looking at the world through the eyes of a child." During this 24-hour period, I won't allow myself to be burdened by thoughts of giants and monsters—of things that are past. I won't concern myself about tomorrow until it becomes my today. The better I use today, the more likely it is that tomorrow will be bright. *Have I extended the hand of caring to another person today?*

Today I Pray

God, may I please grow up. May I no longer see monsters and giants on my walls, those projections of a child's imagination. May I bury my hobgoblins and realize that those epic dream-monsters are distortions of my present fears. May they vanish with my fearfulness, in the daylight of my new serenity.

Today I Will Remember

I will put away childish fears.

Reflection for the Day

Can I be wholeheartedly grateful for today? It so, I'm opening doors to more and more abundant good. What if I can't be thankful for the "rain" that has fallen in my life—for the so-called bad times? What then? I can begin by giving thanks for all the sunshine I can remember, and for every blessing that has come my way. Perhaps then I'll be able to look back over the rainy periods of my life with new vision, seeing them as necessary; perhaps then, hidden blessings I've overlooked will come to my attention. *Am I grateful for all of life—both the sunshine and the rain?*

Today I Pray

May I be grateful for all that has happened to me, good and bad. Bad helps to define good. Sorrow intensifies joy. Humility brings spirituality. Disease turns health into a paradise. Loneliness makes love, both human and Divine, the greatest gift of all. I thank God for the contrasts which have made me know God better.

Today I Will Remember

I am grateful for the whole of life.

Reflection for the Day

As I attend meetings of the Program, may eyes open wider and wider. Other people's problems make mine look small, yet they are facing them with courage and confidence. Others are trapped in situations as bad as mine, but they bear their troubles with more fortitude. By going to meetings, I find many reasons to be grateful. My load has begun to lighten. *Do I expect easy solutions to my problems? Or do I ask only to be guided to a better way?*

Today I Pray

Make the Program my way of life. Its goals are my goals. Its members are my truest friends. May I pass along the skills for coping I have learned there. May my turnabout and the resulting transformation in my life inspire others, as others have inspired me.

Today I Will Remember

May I be grateful.

Reflection for the Day

No matter what it is that seems to be our need or problem, we can find something to rejoice in, something for which to give thanks. It is not God who needs to be thanked, but we who need to be thankful. Thankfulness opens new doors to good in our life. Thankfulness creates a new heart and a new spirit in us. *Do I keep myself aware of the many blessings that come to me each day and remember to be thankful for them?*

Today I Pray

May God fill me with a spirit of thankfulness. When I express my thanks, however fumbling, to God or to another human being, I am not only being gracious to God or that other person for helping me, but I am also giving myself the greatest reward of all—a thankful heart. May I not forget either the transitive "to thank," directed at someone else, or the intransitive "giving thanks," which fills my own great need.

Today I Will Remember

Thank and give thanks.

Reflection for the Day

We come to know in the Program that there is no deeper satisfaction and no greater joy than in a Twelfth Step well done. To watch the eyes of men and women open with wonder as they move from darkness to light, to see their lives quickly fill with new purpose and meaning, and above all to watch them awaken to the presence of a loving God in their lives—these things are the substance of what we receive as we carry the message of the Program. *Am I learning through Twelfth Step experiences that gratitude should go forward, rather than backward?*

Today I Pray

May my Twelfth Step be as wholehearted and as convincing and as constructive as others' Twelfth-Stepping has been to me. May I realize that the might of the Program and its effectiveness for all of us come through "passing it on." When I guide someone else to sobriety, my own sobriety is underlined and reinforced. I humbly ask God's guidance before each Twelfth Step.

Today I Will Remember

To pass it on.

Reflection for the Day

I have much more to be grateful for than I realize. Too often, I don't remember to give thought to all the things in my life that I could enjoy and appreciate. Perhaps I don't take time for this important meditation because I'm too preoccupied with my own so-called woes. I allow my mind to overflow with grievances; the more I think about them, the more monumental they seem. Instead of surrendering to God and God's goodness, I let myself be controlled by the negative thinking into which my thoughts are apt to stray unless I guide them firmly into brighter paths. *Do I try to cultivate an "attitude of gratitude"?*

Today I Pray

May God lead me away from my pile-up of negative thoughts, which make for detours in my path of personal growth. May I break the old poor-me habits of remembering the worst and expecting the most dire. May I turn my thoughts ahead to a whole new world out there. May I allow myself to envision the glory of God.

Today I Will Remember

Keep an attitude of gratitude.

Reflection for the Day

When I first came to the Program, I was stunned by the constant sound of laughter. I realize today that cheerfulness and merriment are useful. As the "Big Book" says, "Outsiders are sometimes shocked when we burst into laughter over a seemingly tragic experience out of the past. But why shouldn't we laugh? We have recovered, and have been given the power to help others." What greater cause could there be for rejoicing than this? *Have I begun to regain my sense of humor?*

Today I Pray

May God restore my sense of humor. May I appreciate the honest laughter that is the background music of our mutual rejoicing in our sobriety. May I laugh a lot, not the defensive ego-laugh which mocks another's weakness, not the wry laugh of the self-put-down, but the healthy laugh that keeps situations in perspective. May I never regard this kind of laughter as irreverent. I have learned, instead, that it is irreverent to take myself too seriously.

Today I Will Remember

A sense of humor is a sign of health.

Reflection for the Day

Am I so sure I'm doing everything possible to make my new life a success? Am I using my capabilities well? Do I recognize and appreciate all I have to be grateful for? The Program and its Twelve Steps teach me that I am the possessor of unlimited resources. The more I do with them, the more they will grow—to overshadow and cancel out the difficult and painful feelings that now get so much of my attention. *Am I less sensitive today than when I first came to the Program?*

Today I Pray

May I make the most of myself in all ways. May I begin to look outward to people and opportunities and wonderful resources around me. As I become less ingrown and understand myself better in relation to others, may I be less touchy and thin-skinned. May I shrug off my old "the-world-is-out-to-get-me" feeling and see that same world as my treasure-house, God-given and boundless.

Today I Will Remember

My resources are unlimited

Reflection for the Day

I will resolve to observe with new interest even the commonplace things that happen today. If I learn to see everything with a fresh eye, perhaps I'll find I have countless reasons for contentment and gratitude. When I find myself trapped in the quicksand of my negative thoughts I'll turn away from them—and grab for the lifesaving strength of sharing with others in the Program. *Do I carry my weight as an all-important link in the worldwide chain of the Program?*

Today I Pray

I pray that God will open my eyes to the smallest everyday wonders, that I may notice and list among my blessings things like just feeling good, being able to think clearly. Even when I make a simple, unimportant choice, like whether to order coffee or tea or a soft drink, may I be reminded that the power of choice is a gift from God.

Today I Will Remember

I am blessed with the freedom of choice.

Reflection for the Day

As I grow in the Program—sharing, caring, and becoming more and more active—I find that it's becoming easier to live in the Now. Even my vocabulary is changing. No longer is every other sentence salted with such well-used phrases as *"could've," "should've," "would've," "might've."* What's done is done and what will be will be. The only time that really matters is Now. *Am I gaining real pleasure and serenity and peace in the Program?*

Today I Pray

That I may collect all my scattered memories from the past and high-flown schemes and overblown fears for the future and compact them into the neater confines of Today. Only by living in the Now may I keep my balance, without bending backwards to the past or tipping forward into the future. May I stop trying to get my arms around my whole unwieldy lifetime and carry it around in a gunny sack with me wherever I go.

Today I Will Remember

Make room for today.

Reflection for the Day

We're taught in the Program that "faith without works is dead." How true this is for the addicted person. For if addicted persons fail to perfect or enlarge their spiritual lives through work and self-sacrifice for others, they can't survive the certain trials and low spots ahead. If they don't practice the Programs they'll surely return to their addiction; and if they return to addiction, they'll likely die. Then faith will be dead indeed. *Do I believe, through my faith, that I can be uniquely useful to those who still suffer?*

Today I Pray

May my faith in my Higher Power and in the influence of the Program be multiplied within me as I pass it along to others who are overcoming similar addictions. May I be certain that my helping others is not simply repaying my debts, but it is the only way I know to continue my spiritual growth and maintain my own sobriety.

Today I Will Remember

The more faith I can give, the more I will have.

Reflection for the Day

For those of us who have lost our faith, or who have always had to struggle along without it, it's often helpful just to accept—blindly and with no reservations. It's not necessary for us to believe at first; we need not be convinced. If we can only *accept*, we find ourselves becoming gradually aware of a force for good that's always there to help us. *Have I taken the way of faith?*

Today I Pray

May I abandon my need to know the why's and wherefore's of my trust in a Higher Power. May I not intellectualize about faith, since by its nature it precludes analysis. May I know that "head-tripping" was a symptom of my disease, as I strung together—cleverly, I thought—alibi upon excuse upon rationale. May I learn acceptance, and faith will follow.

Today I Will Remember

Faith follows acceptance.

Reflection for the Day

When I was drinking, I was certain that my intelligence, backed by will power, could properly control my inner life and guarantee me success in the world around me. This brave and grandiose philosophy, by which I played God, sounded good in the saying, but it still had to meet the acid test: how well did it actually work? One good look in the mirror was answer enough. *Have I begun to ask God each day for strength?*

Today I Pray

May I stop counting on my old standbys, my "superior intelligence" and my "will power," to control my life. I used to think, with those two fabulous attributes, that I was all-powerful. May I not forget, as my self-image is restored, that only through surrender to a Higher Power will I be given the power that can make me whole.

Today I Will Remember

Check for "head-tripping."

Reflection for the Day

"To stand on one leg and prove God's existence is a very different thing," wrote Soren Kierkegaard, "from going down on one's knees and thanking Him." It is my confidence in a Higher Power, working in me, which today releases and activates my ability to make my life a more joyous, satisfying experience. I can't bring this about by relying on myself and my own limited ideas. *Have I begun to thank God every night?*

Today I Pray

May I remember constantly that it is my belief in my Higher Power that flips the switch to release the power in me. Whenever I falter in my faith, that power is shut off. I pray for undiminished faith, so that this power—given by God and regenerated by my own belief in it—may always be available to me as the source of my strength.

Today I Will Remember

Faith regenerates God-given power.

Reflection for the Day

Many people pray as though to overcome the will of a reluctant God, instead of taking hold of the willingness of a loving God. In the late stages of our addiction, the will to resist has fled. Yet when we admit complete defeat, and when we become entirely ready to try the principles of the Program, our obsession leaves us and we enter a new dimension—freedom under God as we understand Him. *Is my growth in the Program convincing me that God alone can remove obsessions?*

Today I Pray

May I pray not as a complaining child to a stern father, as though "praying" must always mean "pleading," usually in moments of helpless desperation. May I pray, instead, for my own willingness to reach out to Him, since He is ready at all times to reach out to me. May I regard my Higher Power as a willing God.

Today I Will Remember

God is willing.

Reflection for the Day

I knew I had to have a new beginning, and the beginning had to be here. I couldn't start anywhere else. I had to let go of the past and forget the future. As long as I held on to the past with one hand and grabbed at the future with the other hand, I had nothing with which to grasp today. So I had to begin here, now. *Do I practice the Eleventh Step, praying only for knowledge of God's will for me, and the Power to carry that out?*

Today I Pray

May I not worry about verbalizing my wants and needs in my prayers to a Higher Power. May I not fret over the language of my prayers, for God needs no language, and communication with Him is beyond speech. May the Eleventh Step guide me in my prayers at all times.

Today I Will Remember

God's will be done.

Reflection for the Day

So many of us suffer from despair. Yet we don't realize that despair is purely the absence of faith. As long as we're willing to turn to God for help in our difficulties, we cannot despair. When we're troubled and can't see a way out, it's only because we imagine that all solutions depend on *us*. The Program teaches us to *let go* of overwhelming problems and *let God* handle them for us. *When I consciously surrender my will to God's will, do I see faith at work in my life?*

Today I Pray

May I, as a recovering person, be free of despair and depression, those two "down D's" that are the result of feelings of helplessness. May I know that I am never without the help of God, that I am never helpless when God is with me. If I have faith, I need never be "helpless and hopeless."

Today I Will Remember

Despair is the absence of faith.

Reflection for the Day

If I believe that it's hopeless to expect any improvement in my life, I'm doubting the power of God. If I believe I have reason for despair, I'm confessing personal failure, for I *do* have the power to change myself; nothing can prevent it but my own unwillingness. I can learn in the Program to avail myself of the immense, inexhaustible power of God—if I'm willing to be *continually* aware of God's nearness. *Do I still imagine that my satisfaction with life depends on what someone else may do?*

Today I Pray

May I give over my life to the will of God, not to the whims and insensitivities of others. When I counted solely on what other people did and thought and felt for my own happiness, I became nothing more than a cheap mirror reflecting others' lives. May I remain close to God in all things. I value myself because God values me. May I be dependent only upon my Higher Power.

Today I Will Remember

Stay close to God.

Reflection for the Day

I've learned in the Program that I need not apologize to anyone for depending upon God as I understand Him. In fact, I now have good reason to disbelieve those who think spirituality is the way of weakness. For me, it is the way of strength. The verdict of the ages is that men and women of faith seldom lack courage. They trust their God. So I never apologize for my belief in Him, but, instead, I try to let Him demonstrate, through me and those around me, what He can do. *Do I walk as I talk?*

Today I Pray

May my faith be confirmed as I see how God has worked through others since the beginning of time. May I see that the brave ones, the miracle-workers, the happy people are those who have professed their spirituality. May I see, even now as I look around, how God works through those who believe in Him.

Today I Will Remember

To watch God at work.

Reflection for the Day

"Perfect courage," wrote La Rochefoucauld, "means doing unwitnessed what we would be capable of with the world looking on." As we grow in the Program, we recognize persistent fear for what it is, and we become able to handle it. We begin to see each adversity as a God-given opportunity to develop the kind of courage which is born of humility, rather than of bravado. *Do I realize that whistling to keep up my courage is merely good practice for whistling?*

Today I Pray

May I find courage in my Higher Power. Since all things are possible through God, I must be able to overcome the insidious fears that haunt me—so often fears of losing someone or something that has become important in my life. I pray for my own willingness to let go of those fears.

Today I Will Remember

Praying is more than whistling in the dark.

Reflection for the Day

As the doubter tries the process of prayer, he would do well to add up the results. If he persists, he'll almost surely find more serenity, more tolerance, less fear, and less anger. He'll acquire a quiet courage—the kind that isn't tension-ridden. He'll be able to look at "failure" and "success" for what they really are. Problems and calamity will begin to mean his instruction, instead of his destruction. He'll feel freer and saner. *Have wonderful and unaccountable things begun to happen to me in my new life?*

Today I Pray

Through prayer, communion with a Higher Power, may I begin to see my life sort itself out. May I become less tense, more sane, more open, more courageous, more loving, less tangled in problems, less afraid of losing, less afraid of living. May I know that God, too, wants these things for me. May God's will be done.

Today I Will Remember

Be still and know your God.

Reflection for the Day

Now that I know I can't use bottled courage, I seek and pray for 24-hour courage to change the things I can. Obviously, this isn't the kind of courage that will make me a strong and brave person for life, able to handle any and all situations courageously. Rather, what I need is a persistent and intelligent courage, continuing each day into the next one—but doing today only what can be done today and avoiding all fear and worry with regard to the final result. *What does courage mean to me today?*

Today I Pray

May I tackle only those things which I have a chance of changing. And change must start with me, a day at a time. May I know that acceptance often is a form of courage. I pray not for super-bravery, but just for persistence to meet what life brings to me without being overcome by it.

Today I Will Remember

Courage is meeting a day at a time.

Reflection for the Day

My courage must come each day, as does my desire to avoid a single drink, a single tranquilizer, a single addictive act. It must be a continuing courage, without deviations and procrastination, without rashness, and without fear of obstacles. This would seem like a large order indeed, were it not for the fact that it is confined to this one day, and that within this day much power is given to me. *Do I extend the Serenity Prayer to my entire life?*

Today I Pray

May each new morning offer me a supply of courage to last me during the day. If my courage is renewed each day and I know that I need just a day's worth, that courage will always be fresh and the supply will not run out. May I realize, as days pass, that what I feared during the earliest days of my recovery I no longer fear, that my daily courage is now helping me cope with bigger problems.

Today I Will Remember

God give me courage—just for today.

Reflection for the Day

When a person wakes up each morning and rises through sweaty nausea to face frightening reality with bones rattling and nerves screaming; when a person stumbles through the day in a pit of despair, wishing to die, but refusing to die; when a person gets up the next day and does it all over again—well, that takes guts. That takes a kind of real, basic survival courage, a courage that can be put to good use if that person ever finds his or her way to the Program. That person has learned courage the hard way, and when that person comes to the Program, he or she will find new and beautiful ways to use it. *Have I the courage to keep trying, one day at a time?*

Today I Pray

May I put the "guts-to-survive" kind of courage left over from my drinking days into good use in the Program. If I was able to "hang on" enough to live through the miseries of my addiction, may I translate that same will to survive into my recovery program. May I use my courage in new, constructive ways.

Today I Will Remember

God preserved me to help carry out His purpose.

Reflection for the Day

"A very popular error—having the courage of one's convictions; rather it is a matter of having the courage for an attack upon one's convictions," wrote Nietzsche. The Program is helping me to get rid of my old ideas by sharing with others and working the Twelve Steps. Having made a searching and fearless moral inventory of myself; having admitted to God, to myself, and to another human being the exact nature of my wrongs; and having become entirely ready to have God remove all my defects of character—I will humbly ask Him to remove my shortcomings. *Am I trying to follow the Program just as it is?*

Today I Pray

I pray that I may continue to practice the Twelve Steps, over and over again, if need be. The Program has worked for hundreds and hundreds of recovering chemically dependent people the world over. It can work for me. May I pause regularly and check to see if I am really practicing the Program, as it is set forth.

Today I Will Remember

Step by Step. Day by Day.

Reflection for the Day

Looking back at those last desperate days before I came to the Program, I remember more than anything the feelings of loneliness and isolation. Even when I was surrounded by people, including my own family, the sense of "aloneness" was overwhelming. Even when I tried to act sociable and wore the mask of cheerfulness, I usually felt a terrible anger of not belonging. *Will I ever forget the misery of "being alone in a crowd"?*

Today I Pray

I thank God for the greatest single joy that has come to me outside of my sobriety—the feeling that I am no longer alone. May I not assume that loneliness will vanish overnight. May I know that there will be a lonely time during recovery, especially since I must pull away from my former junkie friends or drinking buddies. I pray that I may find new friends who are recovering. I thank God for the fellowship of the Program.

Today I Will Remember

I am not alone.

Reflection for the Day

Many of us in the Program share the memory that we originally drank or used other chemicals to "belong," to "fit in," or to "be a part of the crowd." Others of us fueled our addictions to "get in"—to feel, at least for a short time, that we fitted in with the rest of the human race. Sometimes, the chemicals had the desired effect, temporarily assuaging our feelings of apartness. But when the chemicals' effects wore off, we were left feeling more alone, more left out, more "different" than ever. *Do I still sometimes feel that "my case is different"?*

Today I Pray

God, may I get over my feeling of being "different" or in some way unique, of not belonging. Perhaps it was this feeling that led me to my chemical use in the first place. It also kept me from seeing the seriousness of my addiction, since I thought "*I* am different. *I* can handle it." May I now be aware that I *do* belong, to a vast fellowship of people like me. With every shared experience, my "uniqueness" is disappearing.

Today I Will Remember

I am not unique.

Reflection for the Day

If we felt guilty, degraded, or ashamed of either our addiction itself or the things we did while "under the influence," that served to magnify our feelings of being outcasts. On occasion, we secretly feared or actually believed that we *deserved* every painful feeling; we thought, at times, that we truly *were* outsiders. The dark tunnel of our lives seemed formidable and unending. We couldn't even voice our feelings and could hardly bear to think about them. So we soon drank or used again. *Do I remember well what it used to be like?*

Today I Pray

May I remember how often, during my days of active addiction, I felt alone with my shame and guilt. The phony jollity of a drinking party or the shallow relationships struck up at a bar could not keep me from feeling like an outsider. May I appreciate the chance to make new friends through the fellowship of the group. May I know that my relationships now will be saner, less dependent, more mature.

Today I Will Remember

Thank God for new friends.

Reflection for the Day

I considered myself a "loner" in the days when I was actively addicted. Although I was often with other people—saw them, heard them, touched them—most of my important dialogues were with my inner self. I was certain that nobody else would ever understand. Considering my former opinion of myself, it's likely that I didn't *want* anybody to understand. I smiled through gritted teeth even as I was dying on the inside. *Have my insides begun to match my outside since I've been in the Program?*

Today I Pray

May my physical, emotional, intellectual, and spiritual selves become one, a whole person again. I thank my Higher Power for showing me how to match my outside to my inside, to laugh when I feel like laughing, to cry when I feel sad, to recognize my own anger or fear or guilt. I pray for wholeness.

Today I Will Remember

I am becoming whole.

Reflection for the Day

"When I was driven to my knees by alcohol, I was made ready to ask for the gift of faith," wrote AA co-founder Bill W. "And all was changed. Never again, my pains and problems notwithstanding, would I experience my former desolation. I saw the universe to be lighted by God's love; I was alone no more." *Am I convinced that my new life is real and that it will last so long as I continue doing what the Program and Twelve Steps suggest that I do?*

Today I Pray

May God be the ever-present third party in my relationships with others, whether they are casual or involve a deep emotional commitment. May I be aware that if there is real friendship or love between human beings, God's spirit is always present. May I feel God's spirit in all my human relationships.

Today I Will Remember

God is the Divine Third.

Reflection for the Day

Alcoholism is called the "lonely disease"; almost without exception, alcoholics are literally tortured by loneliness. Even before the end of our drinking—before people began to shun us and we were "eighty-sixes" from bars, restaurants, or people's homes—nearly all of us felt that we didn't quite belong. We were either shy, and dared not draw near others, or we were noisy good fellows craving attention and approval, but rarely getting it. There was always that mysterious barrier we could neither surmount nor understand. Finally, even Bacchus betrayed us; we were struck down and left in terrified isolation. *Have I begun to achieve an inner calm?*

Today I Pray

May I know the tenderness of an intimate relationship with God and the calm I feel when I touch God's spirit. May I translate this tenderness and calm to my relationships with others. May God deliver me from my lifelong feeling of loneliness and show me how to be a friend.

Today I Will Remember

God can teach me to be a friend.

Reflection for the Day

"The language of friendship is not words, but meanings," wrote Thoreau. Life indeed takes on new meanings, as well as new *meaning* in the Program. To watch people recover, to see them help others, to watch loneliness vanish, to see a fellowship grow up about you, to have a host of friends—this is an experience not to be missed. *Can I recall my initial reactions when I came to the Program? Do I believe that I've finally come home?*

Today I Pray

As the Program has given life new meanings for me, may I pass along to others that same chance to re-evaluate their lives in the light of sobriety, common purpose, friendships, and spiritual expansion. Praise God for my new vision of human life. Praise God for restoring for me the value and purpose of living.

Today I Will Remember

I value my life.

Reflection for the Day

When I first listened to people in the Program talking freely and honestly about themselves, I was stunned. Their stories of their own addictive escapades, of their own secret fears, and of their own gnawing loneliness were literally mind-blowing for me. I discovered—and hardly dared believe it at first—that *I'm not alone.* I'm not all that different from everybody else and, in fact, *we're all very much the same.* I began to sense that I do belong somewhere, and my loneliness began to leave me. *Do I try to give to others what has been given freely to me?*

Today I Pray

May I begin to see, as the life stories of my friends in the Program unfold for me, that our similarities are far more startling than our differences. As I listen to their accounts of addiction and recovery, may I experience often that small shock of recognition, a "hey-that's-me!" feeling that is quick to chase away my separateness. May I become a wholehearted member of the group, giving and taking in equal parts.

Today I Will Remember

Sameness, not differences.

Reflection for the Day

When newcomers to the Program experience the first startling feeling that they're truly among *friends*, they also wonder—with almost a sense of terror—if the feeling is real. Will it last? Those of us who've been in the Program a few years can assure any newcomer at a meeting that it is very real indeed, and that it does last. It's not just another false start, nor just a temporary burst of gladness to be followed, inevitably, by shattering disappointment. *Am I convinced that I can have a genuine and enduring recovery from the loneliness of my addiction?*

Today I Pray

Please, God, let me not be held back by my fear of recurring loneliness. May I know that the openness which warms me in this group will not suddenly close up and leave me out. May I be patient with my fear, which is swollen with past disappointments and losses. May I know that the fellowship of the group will, in time, convince me that loneliness is never incurable.

Today I Will Remember

Loneliness is curable.

Reflection for the Day

Getting over years of suspicion and other self-protective mechanisms can hardly be an overnight process. We've become thoroughly conditioned to feeling and acting misunderstood and unloved—whether we really were or not. Some of us may need time and practice to break out of our shell and the seemingly comfortable familiarity of solitude. Even though we begin to believe and know we're no longer alone, we tend to sometimes feel and act in the old ways. *Am I taking it easy? Am I learning to wear the Program and life like a loose garment?*

Today I Pray

May I expect no sudden, total reversal of all my old traits. My sobriety is just a beginning. May I realize that the symptoms of my disease will wear off gradually. If I slip back, now and then, into my old self-pity bag or my grandiosity, may I not be discouraged, but grateful. At last, I can face myself honestly and not let my delusions get the best of me.

Today I Will Remember

Easy does it.

Reflection for the Day

When we're new in the Program, we're novices at reaching out for friendship—or even accepting it when it's offered. Sometimes we're not quite sure how to do it or, indeed, whether it will actually work. Gradually, however, we become restored; we become teachable. We learn, for example, as Moliere wrote, "The more we love our friends, the less we flatter them." *Just for today, will I reach out if I need a friend?*

Today I Pray

May God help me to discover what true friendship is. In my new relationships, I pray that I may not be so eager for approval that I will let myself be dishonest—through flattery, half-truths, false cheeriness, protective white lies.

Today I Will Remember

A friend is honest.

Reflection for the Day

I know today that I no longer have to proceed on my own. I've learned that it's safer, more sensible, and surer to move forward with friends who are going in the same direction as I. None of us need feel shame at using help, since we all help each other. It's no more a sign of weakness to use help in recovering from my addiction than it is to use a crutch if I have a broken leg. To those who need it, and to those who see its usefulness, a crutch is a beautiful thing. *Do I sometimes still refuse to accept easily obtained assistance?*

Today I Pray

God make me see that it is not a sign of weakness to ask for help, that the comraderie of the group is what makes it work for each of us. Like a vaccine for diphtheria or polio, the Program and the strength of the group have proved themselves as preventives for slips and backsliding. Praise God for the tools of recovery.

Today I Will Remember

Help is as near as my telephone.

Reflection for the Day

When I have only myself to talk to, the conversation gets sort of one-sided. Trying to talk myself out of a drink or a pill or a "small wager" or just one chocolate eclair is sort of like trying self-hypnosis. It simply doesn't work; most of the time, it's about as effective as trying to talk myself out of a case of diarrhea. When my heart is heavy and my resistance low, I can always find some comfort in sharing with a true and understanding friend in the Program. *Do I know who my friends are?*

Today I Pray

May I be convinced that, as part of God's master plan, we were put here to help each other. May I be as open about asking for help as I am ready to give it, no matter how long I have been in the Program. May the experiences of countless others be enough to prove to me that "talking myself out of it" seldom works, that the mutual bolstering that comes from sharing with a friend usually does.

Today I Will Remember

When I ask for help, I am helping.

Reflection for the Day

We've all had times when we felt alienated, when it seemed we had nowhere to turn and no one to turn to. When we don't know which way to turn, when there seems to be no one to help us, even then we're not alone or without help; the presence of God is always with us. When we need strength or courage or comfort, God is there with us as the help we need. Even before we turn to God, His love reaches out to us; His loving Spirit in us hears our cry and answers us. *Do I truly believe that I no longer need be alone?*

Today I Pray

May I never be alone, even in a place by myself, if I take time to talk to my Higher Power. May God be my companion, my joy, my ever-present help in trouble. May the knowledge of that constant presence fill me with calm, so that I will not fear either the solitude of my own room or alienation in a roomful of people.

Today I Will Remember

Listen for the presence of God.

Reflection for the Day

When we first reached the Program and for the first time in our lives stood among people who seemed to understand, the sense of belonging was exhilarating. We felt that the problem of isolation had been solved. We soon discovered, however, that while we weren't alone anymore, in a social sense, we still suffered many of the old pangs of anxious apartness. Until we had talked with complete candor of our conflicts, and had listened to someone else do the same thing, we still didn't belong. Step Five was the answer. *Have I found through the Fifth Step the beginning of true kinship with my fellows and God?*

Today I Pray

May God help me learn to share myself, my attributes, and my failings, not just as I take the Fifth Step but in a continuing give-and-take process with my friends. May I cultivate an attitude of openness and honesty with others, now that I have begun to be honest with myself. May I remember who I used to be—the child in a game of hide-and-seek, who hid so well that nobody could find her/him and everyone gave up trying and went home.

Today I Will Remember

I will be open to friendship.

Reflection for the Day

Since I've been in the Program, I've learned to redefine love. I've come to understand, for example, that sometimes it's necessary to place love ahead of indiscriminate "factual honesty." No longer, under the guise of "perfect honesty," can I cruelly and unnecessarily hurt others. Today, I must always ask myself, "What's the best and most loving thing I can do?" *Have I begun to sow the seeds of love in my daily living?*

Today I Pray

May God's love show me how to be loving. May I first sense the feelings of love and caring within me and then find ways to show those feelings. May I remember how many times I cut myself off from relationships because I did not know how either to let myself feel love or to show what I did feel.

Today I Will Remember

When I feel love, I will be loving.

Reflection for the Day

Giving love is a fulfillment in itself. It must not matter whether love is returned or not. If I give love only to get a response on my terms, my love is canceled out by my motives. If I have the capacity to give love, then any return I get for it is a special bonus. It is through giving love, freely and without expectation of return, that we find ourselves and build ourselves spiritually. *Have I begun to believe, in the words of Goethe, that "Love does not dominate, it cultivates..."?*

Today I Pray

May I, the inveterate people-pleaser and approval-seeker, know that the only real love does not ask for love back. May God be patient as I try to practice this principle. May I rid myself of pride that throws itself in the way of love. May I discard my silly cat-and-mouse games that have no place in real love.

Today I Will Remember

I will not give love to get love.

JUNE 1

Reflection for the Day

Slowly, but surely, I'm becoming able to accept other people's faults as well as their virtues. The Program is teaching me to "always love the best in others—and never fear their worst." This is hardly an easy transition from my old way of thinking, but I'm beginning to see that all people—including myself—are to some extent emotionally ill as well as frequently wrong. *Am I approaching true tolerance? Am I beginning to see what real love actually means?*

Today I Pray

May God give me tolerance for any shortcomings or sick symptoms or insensitivities of others, so that I can love the qualities that are good in them. May God instruct me in the truest meaning of love—which must also include patience. May I not overlook the faults of those I love, but may I try to understand them.

Today I Will Remember

Love is understanding.

Reflection for the Day

In the process of learning to love myself and, in turn, to love others freely with no strings attached, I've begun to understand these words of Saint Augustine: "Love slays what we have been, that we may be what we were not." More and more, I feel the enormous power of such love in the Program; for me, the words "we care" also mean "we love." *Just for today, will I try to be loving in every thought and action?*

Today I Pray

I pray that I may feel the enormity and the power of the love I find in the Program. May my own caring be added to that great energy of love which belongs to all of us. May I care with my whole heart that my fellow members maintain their sobriety and are learning to live with it comfortably and creatively. May I never doubt that they care the same way about me.

Today I Will Remember

Caring makes it happen.

Reflection for the Day

"The beginning of love is to let those we love be perfectly themselves, and not to twist them to fit our own image," wrote Thomas Merton. "Otherwise, we love only the reflection of ourselves we find in them." As I replace my self-destructive addictions with a healthy dependence on the Program and its Twelve Steps, I'm finding that the barriers of silence and hatred are melting away. By accepting each other as we are, we have learned again to love. *Do I care enough about others in the Program to continue working with them as long as necessary?*

Today I Pray

May I be selfless enough to love people as they are, not as I want them to be, as they mirror my image or feed my ego. May I slow down in my eagerness to love—now that I am capable of feeling love again—and ask myself if I really love someone or only that someone's idea of me. May I remove the "self" from my loving.

Today I Will Remember

Love is unconditional.

Reflection for the Day

"It seems to me," wrote AA co-founder Bill W., "that the primary object of any human being is to grow, as God intended, that being the nature of all growing things. Our search must be for what reality we can find, which includes the best definition and feeling of love that we can acquire. If the capability of loving is in the human being, then it must surely be in his Creator." *Will I pray today not so much to be loved, as to love?*

Today I Pray

God grant me the patience of a lifetime in my search for the best answer to the question, "What is love?" May I know that the definition will come to me in parts as I live life's several roles—as child, lover, parent, teacher, friend, spiritual being. May I be grateful for my experience as an addictive person, which adds a special dimension to the meaning of love.

Today I Will Remember

All love reflects God's love.

Reflection for the Day

The Program teaches me that not too many people can truthfully assert that they love everybody. Most of us have to admit that we've loved only a few, and that we've been quite indifferent to many. As for the rest, well, we've really disliked or hated them. We in the Program find we need something much better than this in order to keep our balance. The idea that we can be possessively loving of a few, can ignore the many, and can continue to fear or hate anyone at all, has to be abandoned—if only a little at a time. *At meetings, do I concentrate on the message rather than the messenger?*

Today I Pray

May I understand that there is no place in my recovery—or in my entire life as a chemically dependent person—for toxic hatred or lackadaisical indifference. One of the most important positive ideas that I must carry with me is that all humans, as the children of God, make up a loving brother- and sisterhood. May I find it hard to hate a brother.

Today I Will Remember

Hear the message. Don't judge the messenger.

Reflection for the Day

Adjusting myself to things as they are, and being able to love without trying to interfere with or control anyone else, however close to me—that's one of the important things I search for and can find in the Program. The learning is sometimes painful; however, the reward is life itself—full and serene. *Is the Program helping restore me to a sane and reasonable way of thinking, so I can handle my interpersonal relationships with love and understanding?*

Today I Pray

May I respect those that I love enough to set them free—to stop controlling, manipulating, scheming, bailing them out of trouble. May I love them enough to let them make their own mistakes and take responsibility for them. May I learn to let go.

Today I Will Remember

Loving is letting go.

Reflection for the Day

Few of us are entirely free from a sense of guilt. We may feel guilty because of our words or actions, or for things left undone. We may even feel guilty because of irrational or false accusations by others. When I'm troubled by a gnawing feeling of guilt, obviously I can't put into my day all I'm capable of. So I must rid myself of guilt—not by pushing it aside, or ignoring it, but by identifying it and correcting the cause. *Have I finally begun to learn to "keep it simple..."?*

Today I Pray

May I learn not to let myself be "guilted," made to feel guilty when I don't consider that I am. Since I doubtless have the dregs of guilt left over from my behavior, I do not need the extra burden of unreasonable blame laid on me. I count on God to help me sort out and get rid of these twinges and pangs of guilt, which whether justified or not, need to be recognized and unloaded.

Today I Will Remember

The verdict of guilty is not for life.

Reflection for the Day

A friend in the Program taught me to look at excessive guilt in an entirely new way, suggesting that guilt was nothing but a sort of reverse pride. A decent regret for what has happened is fine, he said. But guilt, no. I've since learned that condemning ourselves for mistakes we've made is just as bad as condemning others for theirs. We're not really equipped to make judgments, not even of ourselves. *Do I still sometimes "beat myself to death" when I appear to be failing?*

Today I Pray

May I be wary of keeping my guilty role alive long after I should have left it behind. May I know the difference between regret and guilt. May I recognize that long-term guilt may imply an exaggerated idea of my own importance, as well as present self-righteousness. May God alone be my judge.

Today I Will Remember

Guilt may be pride in reverse.

Reflection for the Day

Some of us, new in the Program, couldn't resist telling anyone who would listen just how "terrible" we were. Just as we often exaggerated our modest accomplishments by pride, so we exaggerated our defects through guilt. Racing about and "confessing all," we somehow considered the widespread exposure of our sins to be true humility, considering it a great spiritual asset. Only as we grew in the Program did we realize that our theatrics and storytelling were merely forms of exhibitionism. And with that realization came the beginning of a certain amount of humility. *Am I starting to become aware that I'm not so important after all?*

Today I Pray

May I learn that there is a chasm of difference between real humility and the dramatic self-put-down. May I be confronted if I unconsciously demand center-stage to out-do and "out-drunk" others with my "adventure" stories. May I be cautious that the accounts of my addictive misdeeds do not take on the epic grandeur of heroic exploits.

Today I Will Remember

I will not star in my own drunkologue (or junkologue).

Reflection for the Day

When I least expect it, my keen addictive mind will try to divert me back toward my old ideas and old ways. My mind is expert, in fact, at planting and nourishing negative feelings within me—feelings such as envy, fear, anxiety, or guilt. The minute I spot any of these poisonous feelings rising up, I have to deal with them. If not, the more I think about them, the stronger they'll get; the stronger they get, the more I'll think about them—to the point of obsession. *When negative feelings arise, do I "name them, claim them, and dump them..."?*

Today I Pray

I should know—and may I never forget—that a sure way to let my feelings get the best of me is to pretend they aren't there. Like spoiled offspring, they act up when they are ignored. But also like offspring, they are here, they are mine, and I am responsible for them. May I learn to pay attention to my feelings, even if sometimes I would rather make believe they didn't belong to me.

Today I Will Remember

Name them, claim them, dump them.

Reflection for the Day

Guilt is a cunning weapon in the armory of the addictive person which continues to lurk patiently inside each of us. We can use the weapon against ourselves in many subtle ways; it can be deftly wielded, for example, in an attempt to convince us that the Program doesn't really work. I have to protect myself constantly against guilt and self-accusations concerning my past. If necessary, I must constantly "re-forgive" myself, accepting myself as a mixture of good as well as bad. *Am I striving for spiritual progress? Or will I settle for nothing less than the human impossibility of spiritual perfection?*

Today I Pray

May I look inside myself now and then for any slow-burning, leftover guilt which can, when I'm unwary, damage my purpose. May I stop kicking myself and pointing out my own imperfections—all those lesser qualities which detract from the ideal and "perfect" me. May I no longer try to be unreachably, inhumanly perfect, but just spiritually whole.

Today I Will Remember

I am human—part good, part not-so-good.

Reflection for the Day

Many of us have had difficulty ridding ourselves of the ravages of guilt. In my own case,
during the early days in the Program, I either
misunderstood certain of the Steps, or tried to
apply them too quickly and too eagerly. The
result was that I increased my feelings of guilt
and worthlessness, rather than freeing myself as
the Steps intend. Soon, though, I became at
least willing to forgive myself, and I made a
new beginning. I undertook all the soul-searching and cleansing Steps in our Program as they
were intended to be taken, and not from a
below-ground position of crippling hate and
guilt. *Have I made amends to myself?*

Today I Pray

May I forgive myself, as God has forgiven me.
May I know that if I am hanging on to an old
satchel full of guilt, then I am not following the
example God has shown me. If my Higher
Power, who has demonstrated forgiveness by
leading me to this healing place, can forgive
me, then so can I. May I not begrudge myself
what God has so generously offered.

Today I Will Remember

God forgives; so must I.

Reflection for the Day

I don't believe that the Program and Twelve Steps work because I read it in a book, or because I hear other people say so. I believe it because I see other people recovering and because I know that I, too, am recovering. No longer do I believe that I am "helpless and hopeless." When I see the change in other people and in myself, I *know* that the Program works. When a television reporter once asked the philosopher Jung if he believed in God, Jung replied slowly, "I don't believe, I know." *Do I know that the Program works?*

Today I Pray

Show me the happy endings, the mended lives, the reconstituted selves, the rebuilt bridges, so I will not have to accept on faith the fact that the Program works. May I see it working—for others and for me. May I be grateful for the documented reality of the Program's success. May this certainty help me find the faith I need to follow the Twelve Steps.

Today I Will Remember

The Program works.

Reflection for the Day

Somewhere along the line as we become more involved in the Program, we reach a sharp awareness of the growth-value of honesty and candor. When this happens, one of the first things we're able to admit is that our past behavior has been far from sane or even reasonable. As soon as we can make this admission—without shame or embarrassment—we find still another dimension of freedom. *In my gradual recovery, am I expectant that life will become ever richer and ever more serene?*

Today I Pray

May I know, even as I take that mighty First Step, which may be the first really honest move I have made in a long time, that honesty takes practice. My old, deluded, head-tripping self is as different from the honest self that I must become as night is from day. May I realize that it will take more than just one grey dawn to change me.

Today I Will Remember

Honesty takes practice.

Reflection for the Day

Learning how to live in peace, partnership, and brotherhood—with all men and women—is a fascinating and often very moving adventure. But each of us in the Program has found that we're not able to make much headway in our new adventure of living until we first take the time to make an accurate and unsparing survey of the human wreckage we've left in our wake. *Have I made a list of all persons I have harmed, as Step Eight suggests, and become willing to make amends to them all?*

Today I Pray

May God give me the honesty I need, not only to look inside myself and discover what is really there, but to see the ways that my sick and irresponsible behavior has affected those around me. May I understand that my addiction is not—as I used to think—a loner's disease, that, no matter how alone I felt, my lies and fabrications spread out around me in widening circles of hurt.

Today I Will Remember

Lies spread to infinity.

Reflection for the Day

The Ninth Step of the Program is: "Made direct amends to such people wherever possible, except when to do so would injure them or others." To make restitution for the wrongs we've done can be extremely difficult, to say the least; if nothing else, it deflates our egos and batters our pride. Yet that in itself is a reward, and such restitution can bring still greater rewards. When we go to a person and say we're sorry, the reaction is almost invariably positive. Courage is required, to be sure, but the results more than justify the action. *Have I done my best to make all the restitution possible?*

Today I Pray

May I count on my Higher Power to stop me if I start to crawl out from under my Ninth Step responsibility. May I feel that blessed, liberating wash of relief that goes with saying, out loud, to someone I have harmed, "I was wrong. I made mistakes. I am honestly sorry." May I not worry about cracking that brittle, cover-up crust of my ego, because the inside will be more mature.

Today I Will Remember

Restitution is blessed.

Reflection for the Day

Readiness to take the full consequences of our past acts, and to take responsibility for the well-being of others at the same time, is the very spirit of Step Nine. A casual apology, on the one hand, will rarely suffice in making amends to one we have harmed; a true change of attitude, in contrast, can do wonders to make up for past unkindnesses. If I've deprived anyone of any material thing, I'll acknowledge the debt and pay it as soon as I'm able. *Will I swallow my pride and make the first overtures toward reconcilation?*

Today I Pray

God, show me the best ways to make "direct amends." Sometimes simply admitting my mistakes may make it up to someone and unload my own simmering guilt. Other times restitution may take some creative thought. May I be wholly aware that I cannot take this Ninth Step unless I develop some caring, some real concern about how others feel, along with changes in my behavior.

Today I Will Remember

First I care, then I apologize.

Reflection for the Day

I believe today that I have a right to make spiritual progress. I have a right to be emotionally mature. I have a right to take pleasure in my own company, and that makes me more pleasant to be with. I also have a right to become willing—deeply willing, entirely willing—to make amends to all those I've harmed. Because I can now accept myself the way I am, I can accept other people the way they are—not entirely, but to a much greater degree than in the past. *Have I begun to make friends with God, and thus with myself?*

Today I Pray

May God show me that it's okay to like myself, even while trying to repair old wrongs and rebuild from splinters. May I keep telling myself that I am different, now, I have changed, I am a better and wiser and healthier person, I have made some good choices. As this "new person," may I find it easier to make atonements for what happened long ago and in another spiritual place. May those I have wronged also find it easier to accept my amends.

Today I Will Remember

It's okay to like myself.

Reflection for the Day

The Program teaches us that only one consideration should qualify our desire to completely disclose the damage we've done. And that's where a full revelation would seriously harm the one to whom we're making amends. Or, just as important, other people. We can hardly unload a detailed account of extramarital misadventures, for example, on the shoulders of an unsuspecting wife or husband. When we recklessly make the burdens of others heavier, such actions surely can't lighten our own burden. Sometimes, in that sense, "telling all" may be almost a self-indulgence for us. So in making amends, we should be tactful, sensible, considerate, and humble—without being servile. *As a child of God, do I stand on my feet and not crawl before anyone?*

Today I Pray

May God show me that self-hatred has no role in making amends to others. Neither has the play-acting of self-indulgence. I ask most humbly for my Higher Power's guidance as I strive to maintain a mature balance in interpersonal relations, even in the most casual or fragile ones.

Today I Will Remember

Making amends is mending.

Reflection for the Day

When we take the Ninth Step, we must be willing to be absolutely honest. Obviously, though, indiscriminate "absolute honesty" would blow the roof off many a house and entirely destroy some relationships. We must hold nothing back through deceit and pride; we may need to hold something back through discretion and consideration for others. Just when and how we tell the truth—or keep silent—can often reveal the difference between genuine integrity and none at all. *Am I grateful for the products of truth which, through the grace of God, I have been privileged to receive?*

Today I Pray

May I have the wisdom to know the fine-line difference between tact and dishonesty. In my eagerness to make restitution, may I not be the charmer, the flatterer, or the crawler who insists, "You're so good, and I'm so bad." All are forms of dishonesty and hark back to the role-playing days of my active addiction. May I recognize them.

Today I Will Remember

Tact is honest selectivity.

Reflection for the Day

"Direct" is a key word in the Ninth Step. There are times, unfortunately, when many of us are hopeful that indirect amends will suffice, sparing us the pain and supposed humiliation of approaching people in person and telling them of our wrongs. This is evasion and will never give us a true sense of breaking with the wrong-doings of the past. It shows that we're still trying to defend something that isn't worth defending, hanging on to conduct that we ought to abandon. The usual reasons for sidestepping direct amends are pride and fear. *As I make amends to others, do I realize that the real, lasting benefits accrue to me?*

Today I Pray

May I be sure that the best reward for coming on straight as I try to repair my damages is, after all, my own. But may I avoid making amends purely for my own benefit—to be forgiven, to be reinstated, to flaunt the "new me." Ego-puffing and people-pleasing are not part of the real "new me." God save me from opportunism.

Today I Will Remember

No puffery or people-pleasing.

Reflection for the Day

The minute we think about a twisted or broken relationship with another person, our emotions go on the defensive. To avoid looking at the wrongs we've done another, we resentfully focus on the wrong he or she has done us. With a sense of triumph, we seize upon his or her slightest misbehavior as the perfect excuse for minimizing or forgetting our own. We have to remember that we're not the only ones plagued by sick emotions. Often, we're really dealing with fellow sufferers, including those whose woes we've increased. *If I'm about to ask forgiveness for myself, why shouldn't I start out by forgiving them?*

Today I Pray

When I blame or fault-find, may my Higher Power tell me to look under the rug for my own feeling of guilt, which I have neatly swept under it. May I recognize these behavior clues for what they really are.

Today I Will Remember

Resentment, inside-out, is guilt.

Reflection for the Day

Complacency is my enemy, easy to recognize in others, but difficult to identify and accept in myself. Complacency simply means being sure we're right—taking it for granted that we couldn't possibly be wrong. It means, moreover, judging others by what we think is right. It blocks out understanding and kindness, and seems to justify qualities in ourselves that we'd find wholly intolerable in others. *Do I tend to assume that my views are always correct?*

Today I Pray

God, please steer me past complacency, that state of being on dead center. When I am smug, I am no longer a seeker. If I assume I am always right, I am never on guard for my own mistakes, which can run away with me. Keep me teachable. Keep me growing, in heart, mind, and spirit.

Today I Will Remember

Complacency stunts growth.

Reflection for the Day

The primary purpose of the Program is freedom from addition; without that freedom we have nothing. But that doesn't mean I can say, for example, "Sobriety is my only concern. Except for my drinking, I'm really a super person, so give me sobriety, and I've got it made." If I delude myself with such specious nonsense, I'll make so little progress with my real life problems and responsibilities that I'll likely return to my addiction. That's why the Program's Twelfth Step urges us to "practice these principles in all our affairs." *Am I living just to be free of chemical dependence, or also to learn, to serve, and to love?*

Today I Pray

May I relish and be grateful for my sobriety, which is where all good things begin. But let me not stop at that and give up trying to understand myself, the nature of God and of humanity. Freedom from dependency is the first freedom. May I be certain that there are more to come—freedom from tight-mindedness, from the unrest of bottled-up feelings, from over-dependence on others, from a Godless existence. May the Program which answered my acute needs also answer my chronic ones.

Today I Will Remember

Sobriety is just a beginning.

Reflection for the Day

If ever I come to the complacent conclusion that I don't need the Program any longer, let me quickly remind myself that it can do far more than carry me through the anguish of living in the bondage of addiction. Let me further remind myself that I can make even greater strides in fulfilling myself, for the Program and the Twelve Steps is a philosophy—a way of life. *Will I ever outgrow my need for the Program?*

Today I Pray

May my Higher Power lead me through the Twelve Steps, not just once, but again and again, until they become the guiding principles of my existence. This is no quickie seminar on improving the quality of my life; this is my life, restored to me through Divine Power and the friendship of my fellow addicts, who, like me, are recovering in the best known way.

Today I Will Remember

Step by Step, from bondage to abundant life.

Reflection for the Day

How many of us would presume to announce, "Well, I'm sober and I'm happy. What more can I want, or do? I'm fine just the way I am." Experience has taught us that the price of such smug complacency—or, more politely, self-satisfaction—is an inevitable backslide, punctuated sooner or later by a very rude awakening. We have to grow, or else we deteriorate. For us, the status quo can only be for today, never for tomorrow. Change we must; we can't stand still. *Am I sometimes tempted to rest on my laurels?*

Today I Pray

May I look around me and see that all living things are either growing or deteriorating; nothing that is alive is static, life flows on. May I be carried along on that life-flow, unafraid of change, disengaging myself from the snags along the way which hold me back and interrupt my progress.

Today I Will Remember

Living is changing.

Reflection for the Day

Little by little, I'm getting over my tendency to procrastinate. I always used to put things off till tomorrow, and, of course, they never got done. Instead of "Do it now," my motto was "Tomorrow's another day." When I was loaded, I had grandiose plans; when I came down, I was too busy getting "well" to start anything. I've learned in the Program that it's far better to make a mistake once in a while than to never do anything at all. *Am I learning to do it now?*

Today I Pray

May God help me cure my habitual tardiness and "get me to the church on time." May I free myself of the self-imposed chaos of lifelong pro-crastination: library books overdue, appoint-ments half-missed, assignments turned in late, schedules unmet, meals half-cooked. May I be sure if I, as an addict, led a disordered life, I, as a recovering addict, need order. May God give me the serenity I need to restore order and orga-nization to my daily living.

Today I Will Remember

I will not be put off by my tendency to put off.

Reflection for the Day

Almost daily, I hear of seemingly mysterious coincidences in the lives of my friends in the Program. From time to time, I've experienced such "coincidences" myself: showing up at the right place at exactly the right time; phoning a friend who, unbeknownst to me, desperately needed that particular phone call at that precise moment; hearing "my story" at an unfamiliar meeting in a strange town. These days, I choose to believe that many of life's so-called "coincidences" are actually small miracles of God, who prefers to remain anonymous. *Am I continuingly grateful for the miracle of my recovery?*

Today I Pray

May my awareness of a Higher Power working in our lives grow in sensitivity as I learn, each day, of "coincidences" that defy statistics, illnesses that reverse their prognoses, hairbreadth escapes that defy death, chance meetings that change the course of a life. When the un-understandable happens, may I perceive it as just another of God's frequent miracles. My own death-defying miracle is witness enough for me.

Today I Will Remember

My life is a miracle.

Reflection for the Day

Once we surrendered and came to the Program, many of us wondered what we would do with all that time on our hands. All the hours we'd previously spent planning, hiding, alibiing, getting loaded, coming down, getting "well," juggling our accounts—and all the rest—threatened to turn into empty chunks of time that somehow had to be filled. We needed new ways to use the energy previously absorbed by our addictions. We soon realized that substituting a new and different activity is far easier than just stopping the old activity and putting nothing in its place. *Am I redirecting my mind and energy?*

Today I Pray

I pray that, once free of the encumbrance of my addiction, I may turn to my Higher Power to discover for me how to fill my time constructively and creatively. May that same Power that makes human paths cross and links certain people to specific situations, lead me along good new roads into good new places.

Today I Will Remember

Happenstance may be more than chance.

Reflection for the Day

I've learned in the Program that the trick, for me, is not stopping drinking, but staying stopped and learning how not to *start* again. It was always relatively easy to stop, if only by sheer incapacity alone; God knows, I stopped literally thousands of times. To stay stopped, I've had to develop a positive program of action. I've had to learn to *live* sober, cultivating new habit patterns, new interests, and new attitudes. *Am I remaining flexible in my new life? Am I exercising my freedom to abandon limited objectives?*

Today I Pray

I pray that my new life will be filled with new patterns, new friends, new activities, new ways of looking at things. I need God's help to overhaul my lifestyle to include all the newness it must hold. I also need a few ideas of my own. May my independence from chemicals or compulsive behavior help me make my choices with an open mind and a clear, appraising eye.

Today I Will Remember

Stopping is starting.

Reflection for the Day

Fear may have originally brought some of us to the Program. In the beginning, fear alone may help some of us stay away from the first drink, pill, joint, or whatever. But a fearful state is hardly conducive to comfort and happiness— not for long. We have to find alternatives to fear to get us through those first empty hours, days, or even weeks. For most of us, the answer has been to become active in and around the Program. In no time, we feel that we truly belong; for the first time in a long time, we begin to feel a "part of" rather than "apart from." *Am I willing to take the initiative?*

Today I Pray

May God please help me find alternatives to fear—that watchdog of my earliest abstinence. I thank my Higher Power for directing me to a place where I can meet others who have experienced the same compulsions and fears. I am grateful for my feeling of belonging.

Today I Will Remember

I am "a part of," not "apart from."

Reflection for the Day

During our days of active addiction, many of us displayed almost dazzlingly fertile powers of imagination. In no time at all, we could dream up more reasons—or *excuses*—for pursuing our addictions than most people use for all other purposes in their entire lives. When we first come to the Program, our once-imaginative minds seem to become lethargic and even numb. "Now what do I do?" many of us wonder. Gradually, however, the lethargy disappears. We begin learning to live and become turned on to life in ways that we never dreamed possible. *Am I finding that I can now enjoy activities that I wouldn't even consider in the old days?*

Today I Pray

May God give me a new surge of energy directed toward "turning on to life" rather than making excuses for not handling my responsibilities. May my Higher Power allow my out-of-order imagination to be restored—not to the buzzing overactivity of my compulsive days, but to a healthy openness to life's boundless possibilities.

Today I Will Remember

Turn on to life.

Reflection for the Day

Change is a part of the flow of life. Sometimes we're frustrated because change seems slow in coming. Sometimes, too, we're resistant to a change that seems to have been thrust upon us. We must remember that change, in and of itself, neither binds us nor frees us. Only our attitude toward change binds or frees. As we learn to flow with the stream of life, praying for guidance about any change that presents itself—praying, also, for guidance if we want to make a change and none seems in view—we become willing. *Am I willing to let God take charge, directing me in the changes I should make and the actions I should take?*

Today I Pray

When change comes too fast—or not fast enough—for me, I pray I can adjust accordingly to make use of the freedom the Program offers to me. I pray for the guidance of my Higher Power when change presents itself—or when it doesn't and I wish it would. May I listen for direction from that Power.

Today I Will Remember

God is in charge.

Reflection for the Day

It's time for me to start being responsible for my own actions. It's time for me to be willing to take some chances. If my new life in the Program is valid and right, as I truly believe, then surely it can stand the test of exposure to real-life situations and problems. So I won't be afraid to be human and, if necessary, to sometimes fall on my face in the process of living. Living is what the Program is all about. And living entails sharing, accepting, giving—interacting with other people. Now is the time for me to put my faith into action. *Have I begun to practice what I preach by putting my new thoughts and ideas into action?*

Today I Pray

May the Program, with God's help, give me a chance to live a steady, creative outreaching life, so that I may share with others what has been given to me. May I realize on this Declaration of Independence Day that I, too, have a celebration of freedom—freedom from my addiction.

Today I Will Remember

To celebrate my personal freedom.

Reflection for the Day

I am free to be, to do, to accept, to reject. I am free to be the wise, loving, kind, and patient person I want to be. I'm free to do that which I consider wise—that which will in no way harm or hinder another person. I'm free to do that which will lead me into paths of peace and satisfaction. I'm free to decide for or against, to say no and to say yes. I'm free to live life in a productive way and to contribute what I have to give to life. *Am I coming to believe that I'm free to be the best self I'm able to be?*

Today I Pray

Let the freedom I am now experiencing continue to flow through my life into productiveness, into the conviction of life's goodness I have always wanted to share. May I accept this freedom with God's blessing—and use it wisely.

Today I Will Remember

Let freedom ring true.

Reflection for the Day

Some people in the Program don't feel that they can do the things they want to do. They doubt their own ability. But actually, every person has untapped ability. We're children of God, which should give us a strong clue as to the *infinite* nature of our ability. As spiritual beings, we're unlimited. True, we may find it easier to accept this as true of some person who shines in a particular field. I may compare my own accomplishments with another's and feel discouraged. But the only comparison I need make or should make is with myself. *Am I a better, more productive person today?*

Today I Pray

May I realize that I am a child of God. And His loving-parent promise to give me what I need, not what I might want, is His way of teaching me to be what I am, not what I dreamed I should be. As a spiritual being, I can truly become a productive person, perhaps even do some of the things I once felt unable to do without the aid of props—drinks, pills, excesses of food, which lulled me into false confidence.

Today I Will Remember

To compare me with the old me.

Reflection for the Day

What wonderful things could happen in my life if I could get rid of my natural impulse to justify my actions. Is honesty so deeply repressed under layers of guilt that I can't release it to understand my motives? Being honest with ourselves isn't easy. It's difficult to search out why I had this or that impulse and, more importantly, why I acted upon it. Nothing makes us feel so vulnerable as to give up the crutch of "the alibi," yet my willingness to be vulnerable will go a long way toward helping me grow in the Program. *Am I becoming more aware that self-deception multiplies my problems?*

Today I Pray

May God remove my urge to make excuses. Help me to face up to the realities that surface when I am honest with myself. Help me to know, as certainly as day follows sunrise, that my difficulties will be lessened if I can only trust His will.

Today I Will Remember

I will be willing to do God's will.

Reflection for the Day

When we speak with a friend in the Program, we shouldn't hesitate to remind him or her of our need for privacy. Intimate communication is normally so free and easy among us that even a friend or sponsor may sometimes forget when we expect him to remain silent. Such "privileged communications" have important advantages. For one thing, we find in them the perfect opportunity to be as honest as we know how to be. For another, we don't have to worry about the possibility of injury to other people, nor the fear of ridicule or condemnation. At the same time, we have the best possible chance to spot self-deception. *Am I trustworthy to those who trust me?*

Today I Pray

I pray for God's assistance in making me a trusted confidant. I need to be a person others will be willing to share with. I need to be an open receiver, not just a transmitter. Today I pray for a large portion of tried-and-trueness, so that I may be a better and more receptive friend to those who choose to confide in me.

Today I Will Remember

Be a receiver.

Reflection for the Day

When we make only superficial changes in ourselves, and give only lip service to the Program,
our progress is slow and the likelihood of
relapse great. Our regeneration must take the
form of a true spiritual rebirth. It must go very
deep, with each character flaw replaced by a
new and positive quality. *Am I being completely
honest with myself in uncovering the faults which
hamper my spiritual growth? Am I beginning to
replace them with positive qualities?*

Today I Pray

May God's protective hand lead me out of the
darkness of my deepest fear—that I could return
to being what I do not want to be. Please, God,
give me courage to make an honest appraisal of
myself. Please help me cultivate my positive
qualities and begin to be free of my fears.

Today I Will Remember

I must be reborn in the Spirit.

Reflection for the Day

The Program is a road, not a resting place. Before we came to the Program—and, for some of us, many times afterward—most of us looked for answers to our living problems in religion, philosophy, psychology, self-help groups, and so on. Invariably, these fields held forth the goals that were precisely what we wanted; they offered freedom, calm, confidence, and joy. But there was one major loophole: they never gave us a workable method of getting there. They never told us how to get from where we were to where we were supposed to be. *Do I truly believe that I can find everything that I need and really want through the Twelve Steps?*

Today I Pray

May I know that, once through the Twelve Steps, I am not on a plane surface. For life is not a flat field, but a slope upward. And those flights of steps must be taken over and over and remembered. May I be sure that, once I have made them totally familiar to me, they will take me anywhere I want to go.

Today I Will Remember

The Steps are a road, not a resting place.

Reflection for the Day

Someone once defined the ego as "the sum total of false ideas about myself." Persistent reworking of the Twelve Steps enables me gradually to strip away my false ideas about myself. This permits nearly imperceptible but steady growth in my understanding of the truth about myself. And this, in turn, leads to a growing understanding of God and other human beings. *Do I strive for self-honesty, promptly admitting when I'm wrong?*

Today I Pray

God, teach me understanding; teach me to know truth when I meet it; teach me the importance of self-honesty, so that I may be able to say, sincerely, "I was wrong," along with, "I am sorry." Teach me that there is such a thing as a "healthy ego" which does not require that feelings be medicated by mood-alterers. May I— slowly, on my tightrope—move toward the ideal of balance, so I can do away with the nets of falsehood and compulsion.

Today I Will Remember

To keep my balance.

Reflection for the Day

In many respects, the fellowship of the Program is like a reasonably happy cruise ship or, in time of trouble, like a convoy. But in the long run each of us must chart his or her own course through life. When the seas are smooth, we may become careless. By neglecting Step Ten, we may get out of the habit of checking our position. If we're mindful of Step Ten, however, then we rarely go so far wrong that we can't make a few corrections and get back on course again. *Do I realize that regular practice of Step Ten can help to bring me into a happier frame of mind and into serenity?*

Today I Pray

May Step Ten be the sextant by which I read my whereabouts at sea, so that I can correct my course, rechart it as I am heading for shallow places. May I keep in mind that, if it weren't for an all-knowing Captain and the vigilance of my fellow crew members, this ship could be adrift and I could easily panic.

Today I Will Remember

To steer by a steady star.

Reflection for the Day

These days, I go to meetings to listen for the similarities between myself and others in the Program—not the differences. And when I look for the similarities, it's amazing how many I find, particularly in the area of feelings. Today I go to meetings thinking that I'm here not because of anyone else's addictions, but because of mine and, most importantly, what my addiction did to my spirit and body. I'm here because there's no way I can stay free of my addiction by myself. I need the Program and my Higher Power. *Am I becoming less harsh in my judgment of others?*

Today I Pray

May I stay alert as I listen, just one more time, to Jack or Jill or Fred or Sam or Martha go through his or her tale of woe or wail. May I find, when I listen with the wholehearted attention I want to be able to give, that each has something to offer me to add to my own life-tale. May I be struck once again by our same-nesses. May each sameness draw us nearer to each other's needs.

Today I Will Remember

In sameness, there is strength.

Reflection for the Day

Conditioned as we are by our old ideas and old ways of living, it's understandable that we tend to resist certain suggestions made to us when we first come to the Program. If that's the case, there's no need to *permanently* reject such suggestions; it's better, we've found, just temporarily to set them aside. The point is, there's no hard-and-fast "right" way or "wrong" way. Each of us uses what's best for himself or herself at a particular time, keeping an open mind about other kinds of help we may find valuable at another time. *Am I trying to remain open-minded?*

Today I Pray

May I be enlightened about the real meaning of an open mind, aware that my one-time definition of "open-minded" as "broad-minded" doesn't seem to fit here. May I constantly keep my mind open to the suggestions of the solid many who came into the Program before me. What has worked for them may work for me, no matter how far-fetched or how obvious it may be.

Today I Will Remember

Only an open mind can be healed.

Reflection for the Day

Faced with almost certain destruction by our addictions, we eventually had no choice but to become open-minded on spiritual matters. In that sense, the chemicals and drugs we used were potent persuaders; they finally whipped us into a state of reasonableness. We came to learn that when we stubbornly close the doors on our minds, we're locking out far more than we're locking in. *Do I immediately reject new ideas? Or do I patiently strive to change my old way of living?*

Today I Pray

May I keep an open mind especially on spiritual matters, remembering that "spiritual" is a bigger word than "religious." (I was born of the Spirit, but I was taught religion.) May I remember that a locked mind is a symptom of my addiction and an open mind is essential to my recovery.

Today I Will Remember

If I lock more out than I lock in, what am I protecting?

Reflection for the Day

Long experience has proven that the Program and Twelve Steps will work for any person who approaches them with an open mind. We have to remember that we can't expect miracles overnight; after all, it took years to create the situation in which we find ourselves today. I'll try to be less hasty in drawing judgmental conclusions. I'll hang on to the expectation that the Program can change my entire life as long as I give it a chance. *Have I begun to realize that my ultimate contentment doesn't depend on having things work out my way?*

Today I Pray

I pray for a more receptive attitude; for a little more patience; a little less haste and more humility in my judgments. May I always understand that change will come—it will all happen—if I will listen for God's will. God grant me perserverance, for sometimes I must wait a while for the Program's Steps to take effect.

Today I Will Remember

Patience.

Reflection for the Day

For my own good, I'll go to meetings and participate in discussions with an open mind that's ready to receive and accept new ideas. For my own peace of mind and comfort, I'll determinedly try to apply those new ideas to my own life. I'll remember that the Program offers me the instruction and support I can't find elsewhere. I'll seek out others who understand my problems, and I'll accept their guidance in matters which cause me discomfort and confusion. *Will I try to be willing to listen—and to share?*

Today I Pray

Thank you, God, for bringing the Program into my life, and with it a better understanding of Divine Power. Help me to remember that attendance and attentiveness at meetings are all-important to continuing in this happily discovered way of life. May I listen and share with honesty, open-mindedness, and willingness.

Today I Will Remember

Here's HOW: Honesty, Open-mindedness, Willingness.

Reflection for the Day

Very few of us know what we really want, and none of us knows what is best for us. That knowledge is in the hands of God. This is a fact I must ultimately accept, in spite of my rebelliousness and stubborn resistance. From this day forward, I'll limit my prayers to requests for guidance, an open mind to receive it, and the strength to act upon it. To the best of my capability, I'll defer all decisions until my contact with my Higher Power has made it seemingly apparent that the decisions are right for me. *Do I "bargain" with my Higher Power, assuming that I know what's best for me?*

Today I Pray

May I not try to make pacts with my Higher Power. Instead, may I be a vessel, open to whatever inspiration God wishes to pour into me. I pray that I will remember that God's decisions are better for me than my own fumbling plans, and that they will come to me at the times I need them.

Today I Will Remember

I will not bargain with God.

Reflection for the Day

Many of us come to the Program professing that we're agnostic or atheistic. As someone once put it, our will to *dis*believe is so strong that we prefer a date with the undertaker to an experimental and open-minded search for a Higher Power. Fortunately for those of us with closed minds, the constructive forces in the Program almost always overcome our obstinacy. Before long, we discover the bountiful world of faith and trust. It was there all along, but we lacked the willingness and open-mindedness to accept it. *Does obstinacy still sometimes blind me to the power for good that resides in faith?*

Today I Pray

I want to thank my Higher Power for this opportunity to open my mind; to learn again about faith and trust; to realize that my wanderings did not change God's place within me or God's loving concern for me. May I know that it was my own doing that I lost faith. Thank God for another chance to believe.

Today I Will Remember

Discard the will to disbelieve.

Reflection for the Day

"It is the privilege of wisdom to listen," Oliver Wendell Holmes once wrote. If I try as hard as I can to cultivate the art of listening—uncritically and without making premature judgments—chances are great that I'll progress more rapidly in my recovery. If I try as hard as I can to listen to the feelings and thoughts expressed—rather than to the "speaker"—I may be blessed with an unexpectedly helpful idea. The essential quality of good listening is humility, which reflects the fact that God's voice speaks to us even through the least and most inarticulate of His children. *Does a holier-than-thou attitude sometimes close my mind to the shared suggestions of others?*

Today I Pray

May my Higher Power keep me from being "holier-than-thou" with anyone whose manner or language or opposite point of view or apparent lack of knowledge turns me off to what they are saying. May I be listening always for the voice of God, which can be heard through the speech of any one of us.

Today I Will Remember

Hear the speech, not the speaker.

Reflection for the Day

When we're faced with some condition or situation not to our liking, how can we have faith that all things are working together for good? Perhaps we have to ask ourselves just what is faith. Faith has its foundation in truth and love. We can have faith, if we so choose, no matter what the situation. And, if we so choose, we can expect ultimate good to come forth. *Have I made my choice?*

Today I Pray

May I be grateful for my God-given ability to make a choice. Out of this gratitude and my sense of the nearness of God, I have chosen faith. May the faith, as my chosen way, become strong enough to move mountains, strong enough to keep me free of my compulsion, mighty enough to hold back the tide of temptations which threaten me, optimistic enough to look past my present pain to ultimate good.

Today I Will Remember

With faith, nothing is impossible.

Reflection for the Day

The Program has taught me that the essence of all growth for me is a willingness to change for the better. Following that, I must have further willingness to shoulder whatever responsibility this entails, and to take courageously every action that is required.

> "I am and know and will;
> I am knowing and willing;
> I know myself to be and to will;
> I will to be and to know."
>
> —Saint Augustine

Is willingness a key ingredient of my life and the way I work the Program?

Today I Pray

I pray for willingness to do what I can, willingness to be what I can be and—what is sometimes hardest—willingness to be what I am. I pray, too, for energies to carry out my willingness in all that I do, so that I may grow in the ways of God and practice the principles of the Program in all my affairs.

Today I will Remember

"I am and know and will."

Reflection for the Day

Today I'll try to settle for less than I wish were possible, and be willing to not only accept it but to appreciate it. Today, I'll not expect too much of anyone—especially myself. I'll try to remember that contentment comes from gratefully accepting the good that comes to us, and not from being furious at life because it's not "better." *Do I realize the difference between resignation and realistic acceptance?*

Today I Pray

May I not set my sights unrealistically high, expect too much. May I look backwards long enough to see that my self-set, impossible goals were the trappings of my addiction; too often I ended up halfway there, confronted by my own failure. Those "foiled-again," "I've-failed-again" feelings became monumental excuses to give in to my compulsion, which blanketed my miseries. May I avoid that sick old pattern. May I be realistic.

Today I Will Remember

Good is good enough.

Reflection for the Day

How, exactly, can a person turn his own will and his own life over to the care of a Power greater than himself? All that's needed is a beginning, no matter how small. The minute we put the key of willingness in the lock, the latch springs open. Then the door itself starts to open, perhaps ever so slightly; in time we find that we can always open it wider. Self-will may slam the door shut again, and it often does. But the door can always be reopened, time and time again if necessary, so long as we use our key of willingness. *Have I reaffirmed my decision to turn my will and my life over to the care of God as I understand Him?*

Today I Pray

May I reaffirm my decision to turn my will and my life over to a Higher Power. May my faith be staunch enough to keep me knowing that there is, indeed, a power greater than I am. May I avail myself of that Power simply by being willing to "Walk humble with my Lord."

Today I Will Remember

Self-will minus self equals will.

Reflection for the Day

The slogans of the Program are seemingly clear and simple. Yet they may still have different meanings for different people, according to their own experiences and reactions to the words and ideas. Take, for example, the slogan, *Let Go and Let God.* For some people, it may suggest that all we have to do is sidestep the challenges that confront us and, somehow, God will do all the work. We must remember that God gives us free will, intelligence, and good senses—it is clearly His intention that we use these gifts. If I'm receptive, God will make His will known to me step by step, but I must carry it out. *Do I sometimes act as if surrender to God's will is a passport to inertia?*

Today I Pray

May my "passport" be stamped with "action." May my travels be motivated by challenges I can readily recognize as things to do, not things to watch. I pray that I may make the most of my gifts from God, of talents that I am aware of and some I have yet to discover. May I not "let go" and give up but keep on learning, growing, doing, serving, praying, carrying out the will of God as I understand it.

Today I Will Remember

God meant me to make the most of myself.

Reflection for the Day

Now that I avail myself of the letters H-O-W suggested by friends in the Program—Honesty, Open-Mindedness, Willingness—I see things differently. In ways that I couldn't have predicted and surely never expected, I've come to see things quite differently from the person I was before coming to the Program. I feel good most days. I seldom feel bad, and never for long. Certainly never as bad as I used to feel all of the time. *Is my worst day now infinitely better than my best day previously?*

Today I Pray

May I remember today to say "thank you" to my Higher Power, to my friends in the group and to the whole, vast fellowship of recovering persons for making me know that things do get better. I give thanks, too, for those verbal boosters, the tags and slogans which have so often burst into my brain at exactly the moments when they were needed, redefining my purpose, restoring my patience, reminding me of my God.

Today I Will Remember

How it was.

Reflection for the Day

Over and over, I see that those who make the best and steadiest progress in the Program are those who readily accept the help of a Higher Power. Once they can do that, it's easier for them to get out of their own way. Their problems then seem to resolve themselves in a way that is beyond human understanding. *Do I realize that the effectiveness with which I use the consciousness of God in my daily life depends not on Him, but on me?*

Today I Pray

May I know that my recovery and growth depends on my being in touch with my Higher Power, not just once in a while, but always. It means turning to that Power several times a day to ask for strength and knowledge of His will. When I understand that my own life is part of a Higher Plan, I will be less apt to trip and fall, head off in the wrong direction, or just to sit tight and let life pass me by.

Today I Will Remember

To be God-conscious.

Reflection for the Day

We learn the value of meditation in the Program. As the beginning of the Eleventh Step suggests, we seek through prayer and meditation to improve our conscious contact with God as we understand Him. One of the great values of meditation is that it clears the mind. And as the mind becomes clearer, it becomes more capable and willing to acknowledge the truth. Less pain is required to force honest recognition of defects and their results. The real needs of the whole person are revealed. *Are prayer and meditation a regular part of my daily living?*

Today I Pray

May God's truths be revealed to me through meditation and these small prayers, through contact with my group which keeps me mindful of my need to clear my mind with daily meditation. For only an uncluttered mind can receive God; only a mind cleansed of self-interest can acknowledge the truth.

Today I Will Remember

Meditation is a mind-cleanser.

Reflection for the Day

The feeling of self-pity, which we've all suffered at one time or another, is one of the ugliest emotions we can experience. We don't even relish the thought of admitting to others that we're awash in self-pity. We hate being told that it shows; we quickly argue that we're feel-ing *another* emotion instead; we go so far as to "cleverly" hide from ourselves the fact that we're going through a siege of "poor-meism." By the same token, in a split-second we can eas-ily find several dozen "valid" reasons for feeling sorry for ourselves. *Do I sometimes enjoy rubbing salt into my own wounds?*

Today I Pray

May I recognize the emotions I am feeling for what they are. If I am unable to point them out to myself, may I count on others who know what it's like to be a feelings-stuffer. May I stay in touch with my feelings by staying in touch with my Higher Power and with the others in my group.

Today I will Remember

Stay in touch.

Reflection for the Day

When we first come to the Program, the most common variety of self-pity begins: "Poor me! Why can't I (*fill in your own addiction*) like everybody else? Why me?" Such bemoaning, if allowed to persist, is a surefire invitation for a long walk off a short pier—right back to the mess we were in before we came to the Program. When we stick around the Program for a while, we discover that it's not just "me" at all; we become involved with people, from all walks of life, who are in exactly the same boat. *Am I losing interest in my comfortably familiar "pity pot"?*

Today I Pray

When self-pity has me droopy and inert, may I look up, look around, and perk up. Self-pity, God wills, vanishes in the light of other people's shared troubles. May I always wish for friends honest enough to confront me if they see me digging my way back down into my old pity pit.

Today I Will Remember

Turn self-involvement into involvement.

Reflection for the Day

One of the most serious consequences of the me-me-me syndrome is that we lose touch with practically everyone around us—not to mention reality itself. The essence of self-pity is total self-absorption, and it feeds on itself. Rather than ignore such an emotional state—or deny that we're in it—we need to pull out of our self-absorption, stand back, and take a good honest look at ourselves. Once we recognize self-pity for what it is, we can begin to do something about it. *Am I living in the problem rather than the answer?*

Today I Pray

I pray that my preoccupation with self, which is wound up tight as a Maypole, may unwind itself and let its streamers fly again for others to catch and hold. May the thin, familiar wail of me-me-me become a chorus of us-us-us, as we in the fellowship pick apart our self-fulness and look at it together.

Today I Will Remember

Change me-me-me to us-us-us.

Reflection for the Day

Self-pity is one of the most miserable and consuming defects I know. Because of its interminable demands for attention and sympathy, my self-pity cuts off my communication with others, especially communication with my Higher Power. When I look at it that way, I realize that self-pity limits my spiritual progress. It's also a very real form of martyrdom, which is a luxury I simply can't afford. The remedy, I've been taught, is to have a hard look at myself and a still harder one at the Program's Twelve Steps to recovery. *Do I ask my Higher Power to relieve me of the bondage of self?*

Today I Pray

May I know from observation that self-pitiers get almost no pity from anyone else. Nobody—not even God—can fill their outsized demands for sympathy. May I recognize my own unsavory feeling of self-pity when it creeps in to rob me of my serenity. May God keep me wary of its sneakiness.

Today I Will Remember

My captor is my self.

Reflection for the Day

When I begin to compare my life with the lives of others, I've begun to move toward the edge of the murky swamp of self-pity. On the other hand, if I feel that what I'm doing is right and good, I won't be so dependent on the admiration or approval of others. Applause is well and good, but it's not essential to my inner contentment. I'm in the Program to get rid of self-pity, not to increase its power to destroy me. *Am I learning how others have dealt with their problems so I can apply these lessons to my own life?*

Today I Pray

God, make me ever mindful of where I came from and the new goals I have been encouraged to set. May I stop playing to an audience for their approval, since I am fully capable of admiring or applauding myself if I feel I have earned it. Help me make myself attractive from the inside, so it will show through, rather than adorning the outside for effect. I am tired of stage make-up and costumes, God; help me be myself.

Today I Will Remember

Has anyone seen ME?

Reflection for the Day

The Twelve Steps were designed specifically for people like us—as a short cut to God. The Steps are very much like strong medicine which can heal us of the sickness of despair, frustration, and self-pity. Yet we're sometimes unwilling to use the Steps. Why? Perhaps because we have a deep-down desire for martyrdom. Consciously and intellectually, we think we want help; on a gut level, though, some hidden sense of guilt makes us crave punishment more than relief from our ills. *Can I try to be cheerful when everything seems to be leading me to despair? Do I realize that despair is very often a mask for self-pity?*

Today I Pray

May I pull out the secret guilt inside that makes me want to punish myself. May I probe my despair and discover whether it is really an importer—self-pity with a mask on. Now that I know that the Twelve Steps can bring relief, may I please use them instead of wallowing in my discomforts.

Today I Will Remember

The Twelve Steps are God's stairway.

Reflection for the Day

One of the best ways to get out of the self-pity trap is to do some "instant bookkeeping." For every entry of misery on the debit side of our ledger, we can surely find a blessing to mark on the credit side: the health we enjoy, the illnesses we *don't* have, the friends who love us and who allow us to love them, a clean and sober twenty-four hours, a good day's work. If we but try, we can easily list a whole string of credits that will far outweigh the debit entries which cause self-pity. *Is my emotional balance on the credit side today?*

Today I Pray

May I learn to sort out my debits and credits, and add it all up. May I list my several blessings on the credit side. May my ledger show me, when all is totaled, a fat fund of good things to draw on.

Today I Will Remember

I have blessings in my savings.

Reflection for the Day

Among the important things we learn in the Program is to be good to ourselves. For so many of us, though, this is a surprisingly difficult thing to do. Some of us relish our suffering so much that we balloon each happening to enormous proportions in the reliving and telling. Self-pitiers are drawn to martyrdom as if by a powerful magnet—until the joys of serenity and contentment come to them through the Program and Twelve Steps. *Am I gradually learning to be good to myself?*

Today I Pray

May I learn to forgive myself. I have asked—and received—forgiveness from God and from others, so why is it so hard to forgive myself? Why do I still magnify my suffering? Why do I go on licking my emotional wounds? May I follow God's forgiving example, get on with the Program, and learn to be good to myself.

Today I Will Remember

Martyrdom; martyr dumb.

Reflection for the Day

Sometimes through bitter experience and painful lessons, we learn in our fellowship with others in the Program that resentment is our number one enemy. It destroys more of us than anything else. From resentment stem all forms of spiritual disease, for we've been not only mentally and physically ill, but spiritually ill as well. As we recover and as our spiritual illness is remedied, we become well physically and mentally. *Am I aware that few things are more bitter than to feel bitter? Do I see that my venom is more poisonous to me than to my victim?*

Today I Pray

I ask for help in removing the pile of resentments I have collected. May I learn that resentments are play-actors, too; they may be fears—losing a job, a love, an opportunity; they may be hurts or guilty feelings. May I know that God is my healer. May I admit my need.

Today I Will Remember

Resentments are rubbish; haul them away.

Reflection for the Day

What can we do about our resentments? Fruitful experience has shown that the best thing to do is to write them down, listing people, institutions, or principles with which we're angry or resentful. When I write down my resentments and then ask myself why I'm resentful, I've discovered that in most cases my self-esteem, my finances, my ambitions, or my personal relationships have been hurt or threatened. *Will I ever learn that the worst thing about my resentments is my endless rehearsal of the acts of retribution?*

Today I Pray

May God help me find a way to get rid of my resentments. May I give up the hours spent making up little playlets, in which I star as the angry man or woman cleverly shouting down the person who has threatened me. Since these dramas are never produced, may I instead list my resentful feelings and look at the why's behind each one. May this be a way of shelving them.

Today I Will Remember

Resentments cause violence: resentments cause illness in non-violent people.

Reflection for the Day

As a recovering alcoholic, I have to remind myself that no amount of social acceptance of resentments will take the poison out of them. In a way, the problem of resentments is very much like the drinking problem. Alcohol is never safe for me, no matter who is offering it. I've attended cocktail receptions for worthy causes, often in a convivial atmosphere that makes drinking seem almost harmless. *Just as I politely but adamantly decline alcohol under any conditions, will I also refuse to accept resentments—no matter who is serving them?*

Today I Pray

When anger, hurt, fear, or guilt—to be socially acceptable—put on their polite, party manners, dress up as resentment, and come in the side door, may I not hobnob with them. These emotions, disguised as they are, can be as full of trickery as the chemicals themselves.

Today I Will Remember

Keep an eye on the side door.

Reflection for the Day

On numerous occasions, I've found that there's a strong connection between my fears and my resentments. I secretly fear that I'm inadequate; for example, I'll tend to resent deeply anybody whose actions or words expose my imagined inadequacy. But it's usually too painful to admit that my own fears and doubts about myself are the cause of my resentments. It's a lot easier to pin the blame on someone else's "bad behavior" or "selfish motives"—and use that as the justificaton for my resentments. *Do I realize that by resenting someone, I allow that person to live rent-free in my head?*

Today I Pray

May God help me overcome my feelings of inadequacy. May I know that when I consistently regard myself as a notch or two lower than the next person, I am not giving due credit to my Creator, who has given each of us a special and worthwhile blend of talents. I am, in fact, grumbling about God's Divine Plan. May I look behind my trash-pile of resentments for my own self-doubt.

Today I Will Remember

As I build myself up, I tear down my resentments.

Reflection for the Day

We've been our own worst enemies most of our lives, and we've often injured ourselves seriously as a result of a "justified" resentment over a slight wrong. Doubtless there are many causes for resentment in the world, most of them providing "justification." But we can never begin to settle all the world's grievances or even arrange things so as to please everybody. If we've been treated unjustly by others or simply by life itself, we can avoid compounding the difficulty by completely forgiving the persons involved and abandoning the destructive habit of reviewing our hurts and humiliations. *Can I believe that yesterday's hurt is today's understanding, rewoven into tomorrow's love?*

Today I Pray

Whether I am unjustly treated or just *think* I am, may I try not to be a resentful person, stewing over past injuries. Once I have identified the root emotion behind my resentment, may I be big enough to forgive the person involved and wise enough to forget the whole thing.

Today I Will Remember

Not all injustice can be fixed.

Reflection for the Day

When I dwell on piddling things that annoy me—and they sprout resentments that grow bigger and bigger like weeds—I forget how I could be stretching my world and broadening my outlook. For me, that's an ideal way to shrink troubles down to their real size. When somebody or something is causing me trouble, I should try to see the incident in relation to the rest of my life—especially the part that's good and for which I should be grateful. *Am I willing to waste my life worrying about trifles which drain my spiritual energy?*

Today I Pray

May God keep me from worrying unduly about small things. May He, instead, open my eyes to the grandeur of His universe and the ceaseless wonders of His earth. May He grant me the breadth of vision which can reduce any small, fretful concern of mine to the size of a fly on a cathedral window.

Today I Will Remember

Microscopic irritations can ruin my vision.

Reflection for the Day

"Quiet minds cannot be perplexed or frightened," wrote Robert Louis Stevenson, "but go on in fortune or misfortune at their own private pace, like a clock during a thunderstorm."

In the Program we hear many warnings against harboring resentments, and rare is the person who doesn't occasionally yield to resentment when he feels wronged. We must remember that we have no room for resentment in our new way of life. Rather than exhausting myself by fighting resentment with grim determination, I can reason it out of existence by uncovering its cause with a quiet mind. *Will I try to believe that the best antidote for resentment is the continual expression of gratitude?*

Today I Pray

Praise God from whom all blessings flow. Praise God for our human sensitivity which, although it can feel the smallest, pin-prick hurts, can also feel the warmth of a smile. Praise God for our human insight which can peel the wraps from our resentments and expose them for what they are.

Today I Will Remember

I am grateful for feelings.

Reflection for the Day

The Program's Fourth Step suggests that we make a searching and fearless moral inventory of ourselves. For some of us, no challenge seems more formidable; there's nothing more difficult than facing ourselves as we really are. We flee from one wrong-doing after another as they catch up with us, forever making excuses, pleading always that our virtues in other areas far outweigh our flaws. Yet once we become willing to look squarely and self-searchingly at ourselves, we're then able to illuminate the dark and negative side of our natures with new vision, action, and grace. *Am I willing to open my eyes and step out into the sunlight?*

Today I Pray

May my Higher Power stop me in my tracks if I am running away from myself. For I will never overcome my misdeeds, or the flaws in my character which brought them about, by letting them chase me. May I slow down and turn to face them with the most trusty weapon I know—truth.

Today I Will Remember

I will not be a fugitive from myself.

Reflection for the Day

Step Four enables me to see myself as I really am—my characteristics, motives, attitudes, and actions. I'm taught in the Program to search out my mistakes resolutely. Where, for example, had I been selfish, dishonest, self-seeking, and frightened? I'm taught, also, that my deeply rooted habit of self-justification may tempt me to "explain away" each fault as I uncover it, blaming others for my own short-comings. *Will I believe that personal honesty can achieve what superior knowledge often cannot?*

Today I Pray

May I not make the Fourth Step a once-over-lightly, let's-get-it-over-with exercise in self-appraisal. May I know that, once I take this Step, I must review it again many times until it becomes, like the other eleven, a way of life for me. May I protect the value of my Fourth Step from my old habit of head-tripping and buck-passing my way out of responsibility.

Today I Will Remember

Personal honesty paves the way to recovery.

AUGUST 15

Reflection for the Day

It's often said that you can't tell a book by its cover. For many of us, our "covers" or surface records haven't looked all that bad; it seemed at first, that making an inventory would be "a breeze." As we proceeded, we were dismayed to discover that our "covers" were relatively blemish-free only because we'd deeply buried our defects beneath layers of self-deception. For that reason, self-searching can be a long-term process; it must go on for as long as we remain blind to the flaws that ambushed us into addiction and misery. *Will I try to face myself as I am, correcting whatever is keeping me from growing into the person I want to be?*

Today I Pray

May God aid me in my soul-searching, because I have hidden my faults neatly from friends, family, and especially myself. If I feel "more sinned against, than sinning," may I take it as a clue that I need to dig deeper for the real me.

Today I Will Remember

Taking stock of myself is buying stock in my future.

Reflection for the Day

Inventory-taking isn't always done in red ink. It's a rare day when we haven't done something right. As I uncover and face my shortcomings, my many good qualities will be revealed to me also, reminding me that they have the same reality as my faults. Even when we've tried hard and failed, for instance, we can chalk that up as one of the greatest credits of all. I'll try to appreciate my good qualities, because they not only offset the faults, but give me a foundation on which to grow. It's just as self-deceptive to discount what's good in us as to justify what is not. *Can I take comfort in my positive qualities, accepting myself as a friend?*

Today I Pray

If I find only defects when I look in that Fourth Step mirror, may I be sure that I am missing something—namely my good points. Although my ultra-modesty may be approved socially, may I learn that it is just as dishonest as rationalizing away my faults. Even an out-and-out failure, if examined from all sides, may turn up a plus along with the obvious minuses.

Today I Will Remember

To give myself, if not an A for effort, at least an average B minus.

Reflection for the Day

The Fourth Step suggests we make a searching and fearless *moral* inventory—not an *immoral* inventory of ourselves. The Steps are guidelines to recovery, not whipping posts for self-flagella-tion. Taking my inventory doesn't mean con-centrating on my shortcomings until all the good is hidden from view. By the same token, recognizing the good need not be an act of pride or conceit. If I recognize my good quali-ties as God-given, I can take an inventory with true humility while experiencing satisfaction in what is pleasant, loving, and generous in me. *Will I try to believe, in Walt Whitman's works, that "I am larger, better than I thought; I did not know I held so much goodness..."?*

Today I Pray

When I find good things about myself, as I undertake this inner archaeological dig, may I give credit where it is due—to God, who is the giver of all good. May I appreciate whatever is good about me with humility, as a gift from God.

Today I Will Remember

Goodness is a gift from God.

Reflection for the Day

As addictive persons, self-delusion was intricately woven through almost all our thoughts and actions. We became experts at convincing ourselves, when necessary, that black was white, that wrong was right, or even that day was night. Now that we're in the Program, our need for self-delusion is fading. If I'm fooling myself these days, my sponsor can spot it quickly. And, as he skillfully steers me away from my fantasies, I find that I'm less and less likely to defend myself against reality and unpleasant truths about myself. Gradually, in the process, my pride, fear, and ignorance are losing their destructive power. *Do I firmly believe that a solitary self-appraisal wouldn't be nearly enough?*

Today I Pray

May I understand that not only must I look to my Higher Power, but that I need to trust my fellow members of the group in this Step of self-evaluation. For we mirror each other in all of our delusions and fantasies, and with these facing mirrors, we produce a depth of perspective that we could never come by alone.

Today I Will Remember

To see myself all around, I need a three-way mirror—with reflections from God, my friends, and me.

Reflection for the Day

"How does the Program work?" newcomers sometimes ask. The two answers I most often hear are "very well" and "slowly." I'm appreciative of both answers, facetious as they may first sound, because my self-analyzing tends to be faulty. Sometimes I've failed to share my defects with the right people; other times, I've confessed *their* defects, rather than my own; at still other times, my sharing of defects has been more in the nature of shrill complaints about problems. The fact is that none of us likes the self-searching, the leveling of our pride, and the confession of shortcomings which the Steps require. But we eventually see that the Program really works. *Have I picked up the simple kit of spiritual tools laid at my feet?*

Today I Pray

May God keep me from laying out my defects by comparing them to someone else's. We are, by nature, relativists and comparers, who think in terms of "worse than...", "not quite as bad as...", or "better than..." May I know that my faults are faults, whether or not they are "better than..." others'.

Today I Will Remember

Bad is bad, even when it is "better than."

Reflection for the Day

All of the Program's Twelve Steps ask us to go contrary to our natural inclinations and desires; they puncture, squeeze, and finally deflate our egos. When it comes to ego deflation, few Steps are harder to take than the Fifth, which suggests that we "admit to God, to ourselves, and to another human being the exact nature of our wrongs." Few Steps are harder to take, yes, but scarcely any Step is necessary to long-term freedom from addiction and peace of mind. *Have I quit living by myself with the tormenting ghosts of yesterday?*

Today I Pray

May God give me strength to face that great ego-pincher—Step Five. May I not hesitate to call a trusted hearer of Fifth Steps, set up a meeting and share it. By accepting responsibility for my behavior, and then sharing my account of it with God and one other, I am actually unburdening myself.

Today I Will Remember

My Fifth Step pain is also my liberation.

Reflection for the Day

After we take an inventory, determining and admitting the exact nature of our wrongs, we become "entirely ready," as the Sixth Step suggests, "to have God remove all these defects of character." Sure, it's easy to feel like that and be "entirely ready" on a morning-after, but we know in such desperate moments that our motive may be remorse rather than repentance, induced more by a throbbing head than a contrite heart. The further we get away from the last addictive binge, the better the wrong-doing looks—more innocent, possibly even more attractive. *Am I ready THEN to "have God remove all these defects of character..."?*

Today I Pray

May I be "entirely ready" for God to remove my defects of character. May those words "entirely ready" re-summon my determination in case it should fade with time and sobriety. May God be my strength, since I alone cannot erase my faults.

Today I Will Remember

I am "entirely ready."

Reflection for the Day

So often, in the past, we prayed for "things," or favoring circumstances, or a thousand requests that were really selfish in nature. I've learned in the Program that real prayer begins—not ends—in asking God to *change* me. In fact, that's exactly what the Seventh Step suggests: *Humbly asked Him to remove our shortcomings.* We ask God for help through His grace and the amazing thing is that such a prayer is answered if we truly want it to be. Our own wills are so much a required part of the result that it seems almost as if we had done it. But the help from God is even more necessary; without Him, we couldn't possibly have done it alone. *Have I asked God to help me change myself?*

Today I Pray

May I learn to pray broadly—that God's will be done, that God remove my shortcomings. No need to specify what these shortcomings are; God who knows all, knows. May I learn that details are not necessary in my praying. All that matters is my humility and my faith that God, does indeed, have the Power to change my life.

Today I Will Remember

I ask God to change me.

Reflection for the Day

I heard someone in the Program once read, "Burn the idea into the consciousness of every man that he can get well, regardless of anyone. The only condition is that he trust in God and clean house." That is what Step Seven means to me—that I'm going to clean house and will have all the help I need. *Do I realize, by taking the Seventh Step, that I'm not really giving a thing, but, instead, getting rid of whatever might lead me back to my addiction and away from peace of mind?*

Today I Pray

May I know that if I should give up that key word "humbly," which combines all in one my humility, my awe, my faith—I would once again be taking too much on my shoulders and assuming that the Power is my own. May God in His wisdom make His will mine, His strength mine, His goodness mine. As He fills me with these Divine gifts, there can be little space left in me for looming defects.

Today I Will Remember

Trust in God and clean house.

Reflection for the Day

Some of us, after we've taken the Fourth, Fifth, Sixth, and then the Seventh Step, sit back and simply *wait* for our Higher Power to remove our shortcomings. The Program's teachings remind us of the story of St. Francis working in a beautiful garden. A passerby said, "You must have prayed very hard to get such beautiful plants to grow." The good saint answered, "Yes, I did. But every time I started to pray, I reached for the hoe." As soon as our "wait" is changed to "dig," the promise of the Seventh Step begins to become reality. *Do I expect my Higher Power to do it all?*

Today I Pray

May I not just pray and wait—for my Higher Power to do everything. Instead may I pray as I reach for the tools the Program gives me. May I ask now for guidance on how I can best use these precious tools.

Today I Will Remember

Pray and act.

Reflection for the Day

Without freedom from addiction, we have nothing. Yet we can't be free of our addictive obsessions until we become willing to deal with the character defects which brought us to our knees. If we refuse to work on our glaring defects, we'll almost certainly return to our addiction. If we stay clean and sober with a minimum of self-improvement, perhaps we'll settle into a comfortable but dangerous sort of limbo for a while. Best of all, if we continuously work the Steps, striving for fineness of spirit and action, we'll assuredly find true and lasting freedom under God. *Am I walking with confidence that I'm at last on the right track?*

Today I Pray

May God show me that freedom from addiction is an insecure state unless I can be freed also of my compulsions. May God keep me from a half-hearted approach to the Program, and make me know that I cannot be spiritually whole if I am still torn apart by my own dishonesty and selfishness.

Today I Will Remember

Half-hearted, I cannot be whole.

Reflection for the Day

We all want to be rid of our most obvious and destructive flaws. No one wants to be so greedy that she or he is angry enough to kill, lustful enough to rape, gluttonous enough to become ill. No one wants to be agonized by envy or paralyzed by procrastination. Of course, few of us suffer these defects at such rock-bottom levels. Not that that's reason to congratulate ourselves; chances are, pure self-interest enabled us to escape such extremes. Not much spiritual effort is involved in avoiding excesses which will bring severe punishment. *When I face up to the less violent and less deadly aspects of the very same defects, where do I stand then?*

Today I Pray

May I give myself no back-pats for not committing murder or rape, beating up a rival, robbing a sweets shop, or stealing from a down-and-outer. In all humility, may I understand that these are only more violent manifestations of human flaws I harbor in myself. May God give me the perseverance to change these from inside, rather than just lessening the degree to which I act them out for the world to see.

Today I Will Remember

Change the inside first.

Reflection for the Day

Taking a long hard look at those defects I'm unwilling or reluctant to give up, I ought to rub out the rigid lines I've drawn. Perhaps, in some cases, I'll then be able to say, "Well, this one I can't give up *yet*..." The one thing I shouldn't say: "This one I'll *never* give up." The minute we say, "No, never," our minds close against the grace of God. Such rebelliousness, as we have seen in the experiences of others, may turn out to be fatal. Instead, we should abandon limited objectives and begin to move toward God's will for us. *Am I learning never to say "never..."?*

Today I Pray

May God remove any blocks of rebellion which make me balk at changing my undesirable qualities. Out of my delusion that I am "unique" and "special" and somehow safe from consequences, I confess to God that I have defied the natural laws of health and sanity, along with Divine laws of human kindness. May God drain away the defiance which is such a protected symptom of my addiction.

Today I Will Remember

Defiance is an offspring of delusion.

Reflection for the Day

"Prayer does not change God," wrote Soren Kierkegaard, "but it changes him who prays." Those of us in the Program who've learned to make regular use of prayer would no more do without it than we'd turn down sunshine, fresh air, or food—and for the same reason. Just as the body can wither and fail for lack of nourishment, so can the soul. We all need the light of God's reality, the nourishment of His strength, and the atmosphere of His grace. *Do I thank God for all that He has given me, for all that He has taken away from me, and for all He has left me?*

Today I Pray

Dear Higher Power: I want to thank you for spreading calm over my confusion, for making the jangled chords of my human relationships harmonize again, for putting together the shattered pieces of my Humpty Dumpty self, for giving me as a sobriety present a whole great expanded world of marvels and opportunities. May I remain truly Yours. Yours truly.

Today I Will Remember

Prayer, however simple, nourishes the soul.

Reflection for the Day

Prayer can have many rewards. One of the greatest rewards is the sense of belonging it brings to me. No longer do I live as a stranger in a strange land, alien in a completely hostile world. No longer am I lost, frightened, and purposeless. I belong. We find, in the Program, that the moment we catch a glimpse of God's will—the moment we begin to see truth, justice, and love as the real and eternal things in life—we're no longer so deeply upset by all the seeming evidence to the contrary surrounding us in purely human affairs. *Do I believe that God lovingly watches over me?*

Today I Pray

May I be grateful for the comfort and peace of belonging—to God the ultimately wise "parent" and to His family on earth. May I no longer need bumper stickers or boisterous gangs to give me my identity. Through prayer, I am God's.

Today I Will Remember

I find my identity through prayer.

Reflection for the Day

I'll begin today with prayer—prayer in my heart, prayer in my mind, and words of prayer on my lips. Through prayer, I'll stay tuned to God today, reaching forward to become that to which I aspire. Prayer will redirect my mind, helping me rise in consciousness to the point where I realize that there's no separation between God and me. As I let the power of God flow through me, all limitations will fall away. *Do I know that nothing can overcome the power of God?*

Today I Pray

Today may I offer to my Higher Power a constant power, not just a "once-in-the-morning-does-it" kind. May I think of my Higher Power at coffee breaks, lunch, tea time, during a quiet evening—and at all times in between. May my consciousness expand and erase the lines of separation, so that the Power is a part of me and I am a part of the Power.

Today I Will Remember

To live an all-day prayer.

Reflection for the Day

From time to time, I begin to think I know what God's will is for other people. I say to myself, "This person ought to be cured of his terminal illness," or "That one ought to be freed from the torment she's going through," and I begin to pray for those specific things. My heart is in the right place when I pray in such fashion, but those prayers are based on the supposition that I know God's will for the person for whom I pray. The Program teaches me, instead, that I ought to pray that God's will—whatever it is—be done for others as well as for myself. *Will I remember that God is ready to befriend me, but only to the degree that I trust Him?*

Today I Pray

I praise God for the chance to help others. I thank God also for making me want to help others, for taking me out of my tower of self so that I can meet and share with and care about people. Teach me to pray that "Thy will be done" in the spirit of love, which God inspires in me.

Today I Will Remember

I will put my trust in the will of God.

Reflection for the Day

Based on their collective experience, the Program's founders suggested a prayer to be said when taking the Third Step—and making *a decision to turn our will and our lives over to the care of God as we understood Him.* "God, I offer myself to Thee, to build with me and to do with me as Thou wilt. Relieve me of the bondage of self, that I may better do Thy will. Take away my difficulties, that victory over them may bear witness to those I would help of Thy power, Thy love, and Thy way of life. May I do Thy will always!" *Have I abandoned myself to God as I understand Him?*

Today I Pray

I praise my Higher Power for my freedom to find my own understanding of God. May my life be God's, whether I think of Him as a Father whose hand and spirit I can touch with an upward reach of my own, or as a universal Spirit that I can merge with as the hard outlines of my "self" begin to melt, or as a core of Divine and absolute goodness inside myself. May I know Him well, whether I find Him within me, without me, or in all things everywhere.

Today I Will Remember

I thank God, as I understand Him, for my understanding of Him.

Reflection for the Day

When I wake up, I'll think quietly about the twenty-four hours ahead. I'll ask God to direct my thinking, especially asking that it be free from self-pity and from dishonest or self-seeking motives. If I have to determine which of several courses to take, I'll ask God for inspiration, for an intuitive thought, or a decision. Then I'll relax and take it easy, confident that all will be well. *Can I believe that when I give up my "rights" of expectations, I'll know freedom...?*

Today I Pray

I praise God for being able to praise God, to choose the times when I will seek Him, to find my own words when I talk to Him, to address Him in the way that seems most right to me. May I expect that He in turn must be free of my expectations, to affect my life as He sees fit.

Today I Will Remember

Who am I to try to tell God what to do?

Reflection for the Day

Sometimes, even when friends in and outside of the Program tell us how well we're doing, we know deep down that we're really not doing well enough. We still have trouble handling life and facing reality on reality's terms. We suspect, at those times, that there must be a serious flaw in our spiritual practice and development. Chances are strong that our trouble lies in either misunderstanding or neglect of Step Eleven—prayer, meditation, and the guidance of God. The other Steps can keep most of us clean and sober, free from other addictions, and functioning. But Step Eleven can keep us growing—so long as we try hard and work at it continuously. *Do I trust infinite God rather than my finite self?*

Today I Pray

I pray for a deepening of my spiritual awareness, for a stronger faith in the Unseen, for a closer communion with God. May I realize that my growth in the Program depends on my spiritual development. May I give over more of my trust to God's eternal wisdom.

Today I Will Remember

I will not give in or give up, but give over to the power of God.

Reflection for the Day

Though I have prayed at various times in my life, I realized after several months in the Program that I'd never really prayed properly. I'd always tried to make deals with God, much like a foxhole atheist; I'd always pleaded, "Grant me my wishes," instead of "Thy will—not mine—be done." The result was that I remained self-deceived and was thus incapable of receiving enough grace to restore me to sanity. *Do I see that in the past, when I prayed to God, I usually asked that two and two not make four?*

Today I Pray

May I look back and review how I have prayed before, for specific solutions that I from my earthly vantage felt were best. May I question, in the longer view of time, whether those solutions would have been right, had God chosen to do things my way. In retrospect, may I see that my pleas were not always so wise. May I be content to trust God.

Today I Will Remember

God may not do it my way.

Reflection for the Day

We're often told that alcoholics and addictive persons are perfectionists, impatient about any shortcomings—especially our own. We tend to set impossible goals for ourselves, struggling fiercely to reach our unattainable ideals. Then, of course—since no person could possibly meet the extremely high standards we demand of ourselves—we find ourselves falling short. Discouragement and depression set in; we angrily punish ourselves for being less than superhuman. The next time around, rather than setting more realistic goals, we set them even higher. And we fall farther, then punish ourselves more severely. *Isn't it about time I stopped setting unattainable goals for myself?*

Today I Pray

May God temper my own image of myself as a superperson. May I settle for less than perfection from myself, as well as from others. For only God is perfect, and I am limited by being human.

Today I Will Remember

I am not God; I am only human.

Reflection for the Day

"During acute depression," wrote AA co-founder Bill W., "avoid trying to set your whole life in order at once. If you take on assignments so heavy that you are sure to fail in them at the moment, then you are allowing yourself to be tricked by your unconscious. Thus you will continue to make sure of your failure, and when it comes you will have another alibi for still more retreat into depression. In short, the 'all or nothing' attitude is a most destructive one. It is best to begin with whatever the irreducible minimums of activity are. Then work for an enlargement of these—day by day." *When I'm discouraged by setbacks, am I willing to start over?*

Today I Pray

When I am immobilized by depression, may I set small, reasonable goals—as miniature perhaps as saying hello to a child, washing my own coffee cup, neatening my desk, offering a short prayer. May I scrap my own script for failure, which sets me up for deeper depression.

Today I Will Remember

Goals set too high set me back.

Reflection for the Day

"If you're not all right the way you are," it's been said, "it takes a lot of effort to get better. Realize you're all right the way you are, and you'll get better naturally." Sometimes we find ourselves in a situation so difficult that it seems insoluble. The more we think about it, the more we get on our own backs for our imagined inadequacy to overcome the situation—and we sink into depression. That's the moment to recall a single phrase, slogan, or bit of philosophy, saying it over and over until it replaces thoughts of the tormenting problem—which, in the final analysis will take care of itself. *Do I sometimes forget that the thorns have roses?*

Today I Pray

May I see that God gives us patterns so that we can take comfort in opposites—day follows night; silence follows din; love follows loneliness; release follows suffering. If I am ineffectual, may I realize it and try to do something constructive. If I am insensitive, may my friends confront me into greater sensitivity.

Today I Will Remember

Clouds have linings. Problems have endings.

SEPTEMBER 8

Reflection for the Day

We are told in the Program that no situation is hopeless. At first, of course, we find this hard to believe. The opposites—hope and despair—are human emotional attitudes. It is we who are hopeless, not the condition of our lives. When we give up hope and become depressed, it's because we're unable, for now, to believe in the possibility of a change for the better. *Can I accept this: "Not everything that is faced can be changed; but nothing can be changed until it is faced..."?*

Today I Pray

May I remember that, because I am human and can make choices, I am never "hopeless." Only the situation I find myself in may seem hopeless, which may reduce me to a state of helpless depression as I see my choices being blocked off. May I remember, too, that even when I see no solution, I can choose to ask God's help.

Today I Will Remember

I can choose not to be hopeless.

Reflection for the Day

The longer I'm in the Program and the longer I try to practice its principles in all my affairs, the less frequently I become morose and depressed. Perhaps, too, there's something to that cynical old saying, "Blessed is he that expecteth nothing, for he *shall not* be disappointed, but instead will be delighted daily by new and fresh evidence of the love of God and the friendliness of men and women." *Does someone, somewhere, need me today? Will I look for that person and try to share what I've been given in the Program?*

Today I Pray

May I be utterly grateful to God for lifting my depression. May I know that my depression will always lighten if I do not expect too much. May I know that the warmth of friends can fill the cold hollow of despair. May I give my warmth to someone else.

Today I Will Remember

To look for someone to share with.

Reflection for the Day

Years ago, Dr. Alfred Adler prescribed this remedy for depression to a patient: "You can be healed if every day you begin the first thing in the morning to consider how you can bring a real joy to someone else. If you can stick to this for two weeks, you will no longer need therapy." Adler's "prescription," of course, is not much different from the suggestion that we work more intensively the Program's Twelve Steps to rid ourselves of depression. *When I am depressed, do I keep my feelings to myself? Or do I do what friends in the Program have suggested that I do?*

Today I Pray

May I turn myself inside out, air out the depression which has been closeted inside me, replace it with the comfortable feeling that I am cared about by real friends, then pass along that comfort to others caught in the same despair.

Today I Will Remember

The only real despair is loneliness.

Reflection for the Day

The one thing, more than anything else, that can relieve my occasional feeling of depression is love. I have to keep myself "lovable" in the sense of being able to love others, rather than being concerned with whether others love me. In somehow losing myself in others, emotionally or spiritually, I usually *find* myself. Today I understand what they meant at those first blurry meetings of the Program when they told me that I was the most important person in the room. *Do I say the same thing to other new members today, and mean it?*

Today I Pray

May I know that if I can love others, without expecting to be loved back, chances are that I will receive a share of love in return. It is only my expectation of approval which cancels out the value of my love.

Today I Will Remember

Love is not an investment, but a charitable contribution.

Reflection for the Day

"At certain moments," wrote Coleridge, "a single almost insignificant sorrow may, by association, bring together all the little relics of pain and discomfort, bodily and mental, that we have endured even from infancy." The Program doesn't teach us to pretend that hardships and sorrow are meaningless. Grief really hurts, and so do other kinds of pain. But now that we're free of our addictions, we have much greater control over our thinking. And the thoughts we choose to spend time on during any given day can strongly influence the complexion of our feelings for that day. *Am I finding different and better ways of using my mind?*

Today I Pray

May I thank God for the pain—however insignificant—that magnetizes my succession of old hurts into one large one that I can take out and look at, and then discard to make room for new and present concerns. May I thank God for restoring my sensitivity to pain after the numbness of addiction.

Today I Will Remember

I can thank God for restoring my feelings.

Reflection for the Day

We hear often in the Program that pain is the touchstone of spiritual progress. We eventually realize that just as the pains of alcoholism had to come before sobriety, emotional turmoil comes before serenity. We no longer commiserate with all people who suffer, but only with those who suffer in ignorance—those who don't understand the purpose and ultimate utility of pain. In Proust's words, "To goodness and wisdom we make only promises; pain we obey." *Do I believe that pain is God's way of trying to get my attention?*

Today I Pray

May I understand the value of pain in my life, especially if I am headed breakneck down a track of self-destruction. May I know that pain is God's way of flagging down the train I'm on before it gets to a bridge wash-out. May I be thankful that pain forced me to throw the switch in time.

Today I Will Remember

Pain saves lives.

Reflection for the Day

Until we came to the Program, our lives had been spent running from pain and problems. Escape by way of alcohol or other chemicals was always our temporary solution. Then we started going to meetings. We looked and listened, often with amazement. Everywhere around us, we saw failure and misery transformed by humility into priceless assets. To those who've made progress in the Program, humility is simply a clear recognition of what and who we really are—followed by a sincere attempt to become what we could be. *Is the Program showing me what I could be?*

Today I Pray

I pray for humility, which is another word for perspective, a level look at the real me and where I stand in relation to God and other people. May I be grateful to humility: it is the processing plant through which my raw hurts and ragged delusions are refined into new courage and sensitivities.

Today I Will Remember

Humility restores my "sight."

Reflection for the Day

No one welcomes pain with open arms, but it does have its uses. Just as physical pain serves as a warning that we may be suffering a bodily illness, so can emotional pain be a useful sign that something is wrong—as well as a warning that we need to make a change. When we can meet pain without panic, we can learn to deal with the cause of the hurt, rather than running away as we did when we were actively addicted. *Can I bear some emotional discomfort? Am I less fragile than I once believed?*

Today I Pray

I pray I may be better able to face hurt or pain, now that I am getting to know reality—good and bad. I sincerely pray that the supersensitivity of my addictive days will disappear, that people will not feel they must treat me like blown glass, which could shatter at a puff of criticism.

Today I Will Remember

Throw away my stamp: "Fragile—Handle with Care."

Reflection for the Day

We learn from others in the Program that the best way to deal with painful situations is to meet them head on, to deal with them honestly and realistically, and to try to learn from them and use them as springboards for growth. Through the Program and our contact with a Higher Power, we can find the courage to use pain for *triumphant* growth. *Will I believe that whatever pain I experience is a small price to pay for the joy of becoming the person I was always meant to be?*

Today I Pray

May my Higher Power give me the courage I need to stop running away from painful situations. The chemical was my escape hatch, the trap door I counted on to swallow me when life became too monstrous or villainous to bear. Now that I have locked that door, may I face pain and learn from it.

Today I Will Remember

My compulsion: a trap door—and a trap.

Reflection for the Day

In a letter to a friend, AA co-founder Bill W. wrote, "I don't think happiness or unhappiness is the point. How do we meet the problems we face? How do we best learn from them and transmit what we have learned to others, if they would receive the knowledge? In my view, we of this world are pupils in a great school of life. It is intended that we try to grow, and that we try to help our fellow travelers to grow in the kind of love that makes no demands...When pain comes, we are expected to learn from it willingly, and help others to learn. When happiness comes, we accept it as a gift, and thank God for it." *Can I accept both pain and happiness willingly?*

Today I Pray

God, please help me remember that everything that happens to me has its worth, including the misery of addiction. May I believe that even my dependence was part of God's Grand Scheme to bring me to Him.

Today I Will Remember

All that I am is all that has happened to me.

Reflection for the Day

In every story we hear from others in the Program, pain has been the price of admission into a new life. But our admission price purchased far more than we expected. It led us to a degree of humility, which we soon discovered to be a healer of pain. And, in time, we began to fear pain less, and desire humility more than ever. *Am I learning to "sit loosely in the saddle"—making the most of what comes and the least of what goes?*

Today I Pray

If God's plan for us is spiritual growth, a closer alliance with His principles of what is good and what is true, then may I believe that all my experiences have added up to a new and improved me. May I not fear the lessons of pain. May I know that I must continue to grow through pain, as well as joy.

Today I Will Remember

I hurt; therefore I am.

Reflection for the Day

It's still not exactly a "piece of cake" for me to accept today's occasional pain and anxiety with any great degree of serenity, but I'm increasingly able to be thankful for a certain amount of pain. In the Program, we find the willingness to do this by going over the lessons learned from past sufferings—lessons which have led to the blessings we now enjoy. We can remember how the agonies of addiction—and the pain of rebellion and bruised pride—have often led us to God's grace, and thus to new freedom. *Have I thanked my Higher Power for the miracle of my life this day?*

Today I Pray

When I was helpless, I asked God for help. When I was hopeless, I reached out for His hope. When I was powerless over my addiction, I asked to share His power. Now I can honestly thank God that I was helpless, hopeless, and powerless, because I have seen a miracle.

Today I Will Remember

From powerless highs to a Higher Power.

Reflection for the Day

"When a man has reached a condition in which he believed that a thing must happen when he does not wish it, and that which he wishes to happen can never be, this is really the state called desperation," wrote Schopenhauer. The very real pain of emotional difficulties is sometimes very hard to take while we're trying to maintain sobriety. Yet we learn, in time, that overcoming such problems is the real test of the Program's way of living. *Do I believe that adversity gives me more opportunity to grow than does comfort or success?*

Today I Pray

May I believe firmly that God, in His infinite wisdom, does not send me those occasional moments of emotional stress in order to tease my sobriety, but to challenge me to grow in my control and my conviction. May I learn not to be afraid of emotional summits and canyons, for the Program has outfitted me for all kinds of terrain.

Today I Will Remember

Strength through adversity.

Reflection for the Day

I've heard it said that when God closes a door, He opens a window. Since I started working the Twelve Steps, much of the fear and pain that haunted my life is gone. Some of my defects have been lifted from me, though I'm still wrestling with others. I believe that if I continue to work the Twelve Steps over and over again, my life will continue to improve—physically, mentally, and spiritually. *Am I more willing and better able to help others by working the Steps myself?*

Today I Pray

I give thanks to God for showing me that the Twelve Steps are a stairway to a saner life. As I re-work them conscientiously, my life does get better, healthier, and nearer to my Higher Power. As I continue to live them, may I feel the same gratitude and exaltation of spirit as those who are just now discovering them.

Today I Will Remember

Step by Step, day by day.

Reflection for the Day

For a considerable period of time after I reached the Program, I let things I couldn't do keep me from doing the things I could. If I was bothered by what a speaker or other people said, I retreated, sulking, into my shell. Now, instead of being annoyed or defensive when someone strikes a raw nerve, I try to welcome it—because it allows me to work on my attitudes and perceptions of God, self, other people, and my life situation. We may no longer have active addictions, but we all certainly have an active thinking problem. *Am I willing to grow—and grow up?*

Today I Pray

May God give me courage to test my new wings—even a feather at a time. May I not wait to be entirely whole before I re-enter the world of everyday opportunity, for recovery is ongoing and growth comes through challenges. May I no longer make desperate stabs at perfection, but keep my aims in sight and develop as I live—a day at a time.

Today I Will Remember

Things I can't do should not get in the way of things I can.

Reflection for the Day

On studying the Twelve Steps, many of the first members of the Program exclaimed, "What an order! I can't go through with it." "Do not be discouraged," we're told at meeting after meeting. "No one among us has been able to maintain anything like perfect adherence to these principles. We are not saints. The point is that we are willing to grow along spiritual lines. The principles we have set down are guides to progress. We claim spiritual progress rather than spiritual perfection." *Can I believe, in the words of Browning, that my business is not to remake myself, but to make the absolute best of what God made...?*

Today I Pray

Even if I am an old hand at the Program, may I not forget that the Twelve Steps do not represent an achievement that can be checked off my "things to do" list. Instead, they are a striving for an ideal, a guide to getting there. May I keep my mind open to deepening interpretations of these principles.

Today I Will Remember

Progress rather than perfection.

Reflection for the Day

"Everybody wants to *be* somebody; nobody wants to grow," wrote *Goethe*.

I ask myself sometimes, as we all do: "Who am I?" "Where Am I?" "Where am I going?" "What's it all about?" The learning and growing process is usually slow. But eventually our seeking always brings a finding. What seem like great mysteries often turn out to be enshrined in complete simplicity. *Have I accepted the fact that my willingness to grow is the essence of my spiritual development?*

Today I Pray

God give me patience and the perseverance to keep on hoeing the long row, even when the end of it is out of sight. The principles of the Program are my almanac for growing, even more than harvesting. The harvest will come, abundant enough to share, if I can stick to my garden tending.

Today I Will Remember

Getting there, not being there.

Reflection for the Day

At the suggestion of a long-timer in the Program, I began taking "recovery inventories" periodically. The results showed me—clearly and unmistakably—that the promises of the Program have been true for me. I am not the sick person I was in years past; I am no longer bankrupt in all areas; I have a new life and a path to follow, and I'm at peace with myself most of the time. And that's a far cry from the time in my life when I dreaded facing each new day. Perhaps we should all write recovery inventories from time to time, showing how the Program is working for each of us. *Just for today, will I try to sow faith where there is fear?*

Today I Pray

God, let me compare my new life with the old one—just to see how things have changed for me. May I make progress reports for myself now and then—and for those who are newer to the Program. May these reports be—hearteningly—about "what I am doing" rather than—smugly—about "what I have done."

Today I Will Remember

Has the Program kept its promise? Have I kept mine?

Reflection for the Day

Is freedom from addiction all that we're to expect from a spiritual awakening? Not at all. Freedom from addiction is only the bare beginning; it's only the first gift of our first awakening. Obviously, if more gifts are to come our way, our awakening has to continue. As it does continue, we find that slowly but surely we can scrap the old life—the one that didn't work—for a new life that can and does work under any and all conditions. *Am I willing to continue my awakening through the practice of the Twelve Steps?*

Today I Pray

May I remember how it was when my only goal in life was to be free of my addiction. All the words and phrases I used were stoppers—"giving it up, quitting, cutting myself off." Once I was free, I began to realize that my freedom had more to do with beginning than stopping. May I now continue to think in terms of starters—"expanding, awakening, growing, learning, becoming..."

Today I Will Remember

My stopping was a starting point.

Reflection for the Day

In times past, even as adults, many of us child-
ishly insisted that people protect, defend, and
care for us. We acted as if the world owed us a
living. And then, when the people we most
loved became fed up, pushing us aside or perhaps abandoning us completely, we were bewildered. We couldn't see that our overdepen-
dence on people was unsuccessful because all
human beings are fallible; even the best of them
will sometimes let us down, especially when our
demands are unreasonable. Today, in contrast,
we rely upon God, counting on Him rather
than on ourselves or other people. *Am I trying
to do as I think God would have me do, trusting the
outcome of His will for me?*

Today I Pray

May I know, from the dependencies of my past,
that I am a dependent person. I depended on
alcohol, mood-altering chemicals, food, or
other addictive pursuits. I was inclined to hang
on other people, depending on them for more
than they could give. May I, at last, switch
from these adolescent dependencies to a
mature, healthy dependency on my Higher
Power.

Today I Will Remember

I have more than one dependency.

Reflection for the Day

Now that we're free from our addictions, living life one day at a time, we can begin to stop making unreasonable demands upon those we love. We can show kindness where we had shown none; we can take the time and initiative to be thoughtful, considerate, and compassionate. Even with the people we dislike, we can at least try to be courteous, at times literally going out of our way to understand and help them. *Just for today, will I try to understand rather than be understood, being courteous and respectful to all people with whom I'm in contact?*

Today I Pray

May I never forget my old sponge-like self, who soaked up every drop of affection and attention my family or friends could give me, until they were sapped dry. May I learn to be a giver, rather than a constant taker. May I practice offering interest, kindness, consideration, and compassion until sensivity to others becomes second nature to me.

Today I Will Remember

Giving is part of being.

Reflection for the Day

In our first weeks or months in the Program, our shaky emotional condition sometimes affects our feelings toward old friends and family. For many of us, these relationships heal quickly in the initial stages of our recovery. For others, a time of "touchiness" seems to persist; now that we're no longer drinking or using other chemicals, we have to sort out our feelings about spouses, children, relatives, employers, fellow workers, and even neighbors. Experience in the Program over the years has taught me that we should avoid making important decisions early in our recovery—especially emotion-charged decisions about people. *Am I becoming better equipped to relate maturely to other people?*

Today I Pray

May God help me through the edginess, the confusion of re-feeling and re-thinking my relationships, the getting it all together stages of my recovery. May I not rush into new relationships or new situations that demand an investment of my emotions—not yet.

Today I Will Remember

No entangling alliances too soon.

Reflection for the Day

No matter what other people do or don't do, we have to remain sober and free from other addictions for ourselves. When our program of recovery becomes contingent on the actions or inactions of another person—especially someone with whom we're emotionally involved—the results are invariably disastrous. We also need to remember that intense dislike is as much an emotional involvement as new-found romantic love. In short, we have to cool *any* risky emotional involvements in the first few months of our recovery, trying to accept the fact that our feelings could change quickly and dramatically. Our watchword must be First Things First, concentrating on our number one problem before anything else. *Am I building a firm foundation while steering clear of slippery emotional areas?*

Today I Pray

May I always remember that healthy relationships with people are necessary for my recovery. But—that substituting an obsession with either a love or hate object is as dangerous to my well-being as any other addiction.

Today I Will Remember

A dependency is a dependency is a dependency.

Reflection for the Day

We can be surrounded by people and still feel lonely. We can be all by ourselves and still feel happy and content. What makes the difference? We feel lonely if we look to other people for something they really can't provide. No one else can give us peace of mind, an inner sense of acceptance, and serenity. And when we find ourselves alone, we needn't feel lonely. God is with us; His presence is like a warm shawl enfolding us. The more we're aware of ourselves as beloved by God, the more we're able to feel content and secure—whether we're with others or alone. *Am I experiencing a sense of God and His love at all times and in all places?*

Today I Pray

May I understand that we each have our own kind of loneliness—whether we are young and friendless, old and kept waiting by death, bereft, left, running away, or just feeling out of it in a crowd. May my loneliness be eased a bit by the fact that loneliness is, indeed, a universal feeling that everyone knows firsthand—even though some lives seem more empty than others. May I—and all the lonely people—take comfort in the companionship of God.

Today I Will Remember

Shared loneliness is less lonely.

Reflection for the Day

An entire philosophy of life is condensed in the slogan, *Live and Let Live.* First we're urged to live fully, richly, and happily—to fulfill our destiny with the joy that comes from doing well whatever we do. Then comes a more difficult challenge: *Let live.* This means accepting the right of every other person to live as he or she wishes, without criticism or judgment from us. The slogan rules out contempt for those who don't think as we do. It also warns against resentments, reminding us not to interpret other people's actions as intentional injuries to us. *Am I becoming less tempted to involve my mind with thoughts of how others act or live?*

Today I Pray

May I live my life to the fullest, understanding that pure pleasure-seeking is not pleasure-finding, but that God's goodness is here to be shared. May I partake of it. May I learn not to take over the responsibility for another's adult decisions; that is my old controlling self trying, just one more time, to be the executive director of other people's lives.

Today I Will Remember

Live and let live.

Reflection for the Day

I've learned in the Program that I'm wholly powerless over my addiction. At long last, I've conceded my powerlessness; as a result, my life has taken a 180-degree turn for the better. However, I *do* have a power, derived from God, to change my own life. I've learned that *acceptance* does not mean *submission* to an unpleasant or degrading situation. It means accepting the reality of the situation and then deciding what, if anything, I can and will do about it. *Have I stopped trying to control the uncontrollable? Am I gaining the courage to change the things I can?*

Today I Pray

I ask my Higher Power for direction as I learn to sort out the things I can change from the things I can't, for that sorting process does, indeed, require God-given wisdom. May "the things I cannot change" not give me an excuse for inaction. May "the things I can" not include managing other people's lives. May I start to understand my own reality.

Today I Will Remember

Acceptance is not inaction. Change is not domination

Reflection for the Day

We are powerless over our addictions; that admission brought us to the Program, where we learn through unconditional surrender that there is victory in defeat. After a time, we learn in Twelfth Step work that we're not only powerless over our own addiction, but over the addictions of others. We cannot *will* another person to sobriety, for example, any more than we can hold back the sunset. We may minister to another person's physical needs; we may share with him, cry with him, and take him to meetings. But we cannot get inside his head and push some sort of magic button that will make him—or her—take the all-important First Step. *Do I still sometimes try to play God?*

Today I Pray

May I understand my all-too-human need to be the boss, have the upper hand, be the final authority—even in the humbling business of my own addiction. May I see how easy it would be to become a big-shot Twelfth Stepper. May I also see that, no matter how much I care and want to help, I have no control over another's addiction—any more than someone else has control over mine.

Today I Will Remember

I cannot engineer another's sobriety.

Reflection for the Day

Soon after I came to the Program, I found a Higher Power whom I choose to call God. I've come to believe that He has all power; if I stay close to Him and do His work well, He provides me not with what I think I want, but with what I *need*. Gradually, I'm becoming less interested in myself and my little schemes; at the same time, I'm becoming more interested in seeing what I can contribute to others and to life. *As I become more conscious of God's presence, am I beginning to lose my self-centered fears?*

Today I Pray

May I see that the single most evident change in myself—beyond my own inner sense of peace—is that I have come out from behind my phony castle walls, dropped the drawbridge that leads into my real village and crossed it. I am back among people again, interested in them, caring what happens to them. May I find my joy here in this peopled reality, now that I have left behind those old self-protective fears and illusions of my own uniqueness.

Today I Will Remember

What is life without people?

Reflection for the Day

As we "keep coming back" to meetings, we're able to recognize those people who have an abundance of serenity. We are drawn to such people. To our surprise, we sometimes find that those who seem most grateful for today's blessings are the very ones who have the most serious and continuing problems at home or at work. Yet they have the courage to turn away from such problems, actively seeking to learn and help others in the Program. How have they gotten this serenity? It must be because they depend less on themselves and their own limited resources—and more on a Power greater than themselves in whom they have confidence. *Am I acquiring the gift of serenity? Have my actions begun to reflect my inner faith?*

Today I Pray

May I never cease to be awed by the serenity I see in others in my group—a serenity which manifests their comfortable surrender to a Higher Power. May I learn from them that peace of mind is possible even in the thick of trouble. May I, too, learn that I need to pull back from my problems now and then and draw upon the God-provided pool of serenity within myself.

Today I Will Remember

Serenity is surrender to God's plan.

Reflection for the Day

When I first read the Serenity Prayer, the word "serenity" itself seemed like an impossibility. At the time, the word conjured up images of lethargy, apathy, resignation, or grim-faced endurance; it hardly seemed a desirable goal. But I've since found that serenity means none of those things. Serenity for me today is simply a clear-eyed and realistic way of seeing the world, accompanied by inner peace and strength. My favorite definition is, "Serenity is like a gyroscope that lets us keep our balance no matter what turbulence swirls around us." *Is that a state of mind worth aiming for?*

Today I Pray

May I notice that "serenity" comes first, ahead of "courage" and "wisdom," in the sequence of the Serenity Prayer. May I believe that "serenity" must also come first in my life. I must have the balance, realistic outlook, and acceptance that is part of this blessing of serenity before I can go on to the kind of action and decision-making that will bring order to my existence.

Today I Will Remember

Serenity comes first.

Reflection for the Day

Determination—our clenched-jaw resolve that we can *do something* about everything—is perhaps the greatest hindrance to achieving serenity. Our old tapes tell us, "The difficult can be done immediately; the impossible will take a little longer." So we tighten up and prepare ourselves for battle, even though we know from long experience that our own will dooms us in advance to failure. Over and over we are told in the Program that we must "Let Go and Let God." And we eventually do find serenity when we put aside our own will while accepting His will for us. *Am I learning to relax my stubborn grip? Do I allow the solutions to unfold by themselves?*

Today I Pray

May I loosen my tight jaw, my tight fists, my general uptightness—outward indications of the "do it myself" syndrome which has gotten me into trouble before. May I know from experience that this attitude—of "keep a grip on yourself" and on everybody else, too—is accompanied by impatience and followed by frustration. May I merge my own will with the greater will of God.

Today I Will Remember

Let up on the strangle hold.

Reflection for the Day

I remember once hearing someone in the Program say, "Life is a series of agreeings or dis-agreeings with the universe." There is much truth in that statement, for I'm only a small cog in the machinery of the universe. When I try to run things my way, I'll experience only frus-tration and a sense of failure. If, instead, I learn to let go, success will assuredly be mine. Then I'll have time to count my blessings, work on my shortcomings, and live fully and richly in the Now. *Do I believe that what I am meant to know will come to my knowledge if I practice the Eleventh Step—praying only for the knowledge of God's will for me and the power to carry that out?*

Today I Pray

May I take my direction from the Eleventh Step—and not fall into my usual habit of mak-ing itemized lists for God of all my pleas and entreaties and complaints. May I no longer sec-ond-guess God with my specific solutions, but pray only that His will be done. May I count my blessings instead of my beseechings.

Today I Will Remember

Stop list-making for God.

Reflection for the Day

When we allow our Higher Power to take charge, without reservations on our part, we stop being "anxious." When we're not anxious about some person or situation, that doesn't mean we're disinterested or have stopped caring. Just the opposite is true. We can be interested and caring *without* being anxious or fearful. The poised, calm, and faith-filled person brings something positive to every situation. He or she is able to do the things that are necessary and helpful. *Do I realize how much better prepared I am to do wise and loving things if I banish anxious thoughts and know that God is in charge?*

Today I Pray

I pray that I may be rid of the anxiety which I have equated in my mind with really caring about people. May I know that anxiety is not an item of outerwear that can be doffed like a cap. May I know that I must have serenity within myself and confidence that God can do a better job than I can—and then my anxiety will lessen.

Today I Will Remember

Anxiety never solved anything.

Reflection for the Day

When I say the Serenity Prayer, sometimes over and over, I occasionally lose sight of the prayer's meaning even as I repeat its words. So I try to think of the meaning of each phrase as I say it, whether aloud or silently. As I concentrate on the meaning, my understanding grows, along with my capability to realize the difference between what I can change, and what I cannot. *Do I see that most improvements in my life will come from changing my own attitudes and actions?*

Today I Pray

May my Higher Power show me new and deeper meanings in the Serenity Prayer each time I say it. As I apply it to my life's situations and relationships, may its truth be underlined for me again and again. May I realize that serenity, courage, and wisdom are all that I need to cope with value unless they grow out of my trust in a Higher Power.

Today I Will Remember

God's formula for living: serenity, courage, and wisdom.

Reflection for the Day

Many people we meet in the Program radiate a kind of special glow—a joy in living that shows in their faces and bearing. They've put aside alcohol and other mood-altering chemicals and have progressed to the point where they're "high" on life itself. Their confidence and enthusiasm are contagious—especially to those who are new in the Program. The astonishing thing to newcomers is that those same joyous people also were once heavily burdened. The miracle of their before-and-after stories and new outlook is living proof that the Program works. *Does my progress in the Program serve to carry the message to others?*

Today I Pray

I pray that my own transformation through the Program—from burdened to unburdened, beaten down to upbeat, careless to caring, tyrannized by chemicals to chemically free—will be as much inspiration for newcomers as the dramatic changes in others' lives have been for me. May I—like those other joyous ones in the fellowship—learn how to be "high on life."

Today I Will Remember

Life is the greatest "high" of them all.

Reflection for the Day

My progress in recovery depends in large measure on my attitude, and my attitude is up to me. It's the way I decide to look at things. Nobody can force an attitude on me. For me, a good attitude is a point of view unclouded by self-pity and resentments. There will be stumbling blocks in my path, without a doubt. But the Program has taught me that stumbling blocks can be turned into stepping stones for growth. *Do I believe, as Tennyson put it, "that men may rise on stepping stones of their dead selves to higher things..."?*

Today I Pray

May God help me cultivate a healthy attitude toward myself, the Program, and other people. God, keep me from losing my spiritual stabilizers, which keep me level in purpose and outlook. Let me ignore self-pity, discouragement, and my tendency to overdramatize. Let no dead weight burden throw me out of balance.

Today I Will Remember

I can't be discouraged with God on my side.

Reflection for the Day

"Fundamental progress has to do with the rein-terpretation of basic ideas," wrote Alfred North Whitehead. When we review the ups and downs of our recovery in the Program, we can see that truth of that statement. We make progress each time we get rid of an old idea, each time we uncover a character defect, each time we become ready to have that defect removed and then humbly ask God to remove it. We make progress, one day at a time, as we shun the first drink, the first pill, the first addictive act that will so quickly swerve us from the path of despair. *Have I considered the progress I've made since I've come to the Program?*

Today I Pray

May I remember that there are few new ideas in this world, only old ones reinterpreted and restated. May I be always conscious that even the big things in life—like love, brotherhood, God, sobriety—become more finely defined in each human life. So may the Twelve Steps of the Program be redefined in each of our lives, as we keep in mind that, basically, these are time-tried principles—which work.

Today I Will Remember

The Twelve Steps work.

Reflection for the Day

All too often I unwittingly—and even unconsciously—set standards for others in the
Program. Worse yet, I expect those standards to
be met. I go so far, on occasion, to decide what
progress other people should make in *their*
recoveries, and how *their* attitudes and actions
should change. Not surprisingly, when things
don't work out the way I expect, I become frustrated and even angry. I have to learn to leave
others to God. I have to learn neither to
demand nor expect changes in others, concentrating solely on my own shortcomings.
Finally, I mustn't look for perfection in another
human being until I've achieved perfection
myself. *Can I ever be perfect?*

Today I Pray

May God ask me to step down immediately if I
start to climb up on any of these high places:
on my podium, as the know-it-all scholar; on
my soapbox, as the leader who's out to change
the world; into my pulpit, as the holier-than-
thou-could-possibly-be messenger of God; into
the seat of judgment, as the gavel-banging
upholder of the law. May God please keep me
from vesting myself with all this unwarranted
authority and keep me humble.

Today I Will Remember

A heavy hand is not a helping hand.

Reflection for the Day

Someone once said that the mind's direction is more important than its progress. If my direction is correct, then progress is sure to follow. We first come to the Program to receive something for ourselves, but soon learn that we receive most bountifully when we give to others. If the direction of my mind is to give rather than to receive, then I'll benefit beyond my greatest expectations. The more I give of myself and the more generously I open my heart and mind to others, the more growth and progress I'll achieve. *Am I learning not to measure my giving against my getting, accepting that the act of giving is its own reward?*

Today I Pray

May I not lose sight of that Pillar of the Program—helping myself through helping others in our purpose of achieving comfortable sobriety. May I feel that marvel of giving and taking and giving back again from the moment I take the First Step. May I care deeply about others' maintaining their freedom from chemicals, and may I know that they care about me. It is a simple—and beautiful—exchange.

Today I Will Remember

Give and take and give back again.

Reflection for the Day

Now that we're sober and living in reality, it's sometimes difficult to see ourselves as others see us and, in the process, determine how much progress we've made in recovery. In the old days, the back-of-the-bar mirror presented us with a distorted and illusory view of ourselves: The way we imagined ourselves to be and the way we imagined ourselves to appear in the eyes of others. A good way for me to measure my progress today is simply to look about me at my friends in the Program. As I witness the miracle of their recoveries, I realize that I'm part of the same miracle—and will remain so as long as I'm willing. *Am I grateful for reality and the Divine miracle of my recovery?*

Today I Pray

May God keep my eyes open for miracles—those marvelous changes that have taken place in my own life and in the lives of my friends in the group. May I ask no other measurement of progress than a smile I can honestly mean and a clear eye and a mind that can, at last, touch reality. May my own joy be my answer to my question, "How am I doing?"

Today I Will Remember

Miracles measure our progress. Who needs more?

OCTOBER 18

Reflection for the Day

Not in my wildest dreams could I have imagined the rewards that would be mine when I first contemplated turning my life and will over to the care of God as I understand Him. Now I can rejoice in the blessing of my own recovery, as well as the recoveries of countless others who have found hope and a new way of life in the Program. After all the years of waste and terror, I realize today that God has always been on my side and at my side. *Isn't my clearer understanding of God's will one of the best things that has happened to me?*

Today I Pray

May I be thankful for the blessed contrast between the way my life used to be (Part I) and the way it is now (Part II). In Part I, I was the practicing addict, adrift among my fears and delusions. In Part II, I am the recovering addict, rediscovering my emotions, accepting my responsibilities, learning what the real world has to offer Without the contrast, I could never feel the joy I know today or sense the peaceful nearness of my Higher Power.

Today I Will Remember

I am grateful for such contrast.

Reflection for the Day

There are countless ways by which my progress and growth in the Program can be measured. One of the most important is my awareness that I'm no longer compelled, almost obsessively, to go around judging everything and everybody. My only business today is to work on changing myself, rather than other people, places, and things. In its own way, the obsession of being forever judgmental was as burdensome to me as the obsession of my addiction; I'm grateful that both weights have been lifted from my shoulders. *When I become judgmental, will I remind myself that I'm trespassing on God's territory?*

Today I Pray

Forgive me my trespasses, when I have become the self-proclaimed judge-and-jury of my peers. By being judgmental, I have trespassed on the rights of others to judge themselves—and on the rights of God in the Highest Court of all. May I throw away all my judgmental tools—my own yardstick and measuring tapes, my own comparisons, my unreachable standards—and accept each person as an individual beyond compare.

Today I Will Remember

Throw away old tapes—especially measuring tapes.

Reflection for the Day

Before I admitted my powerlessness over alcohol and other chemicals, I had as much self-worth as a "peeled zero." I came into the Program as a nobody who desperately wanted to be a somebody. In retrospect, my self-esteem was shredded, seemingly beyond repair. Gradually, the Program has enabled me to achieve an ever stronger sense of self-worth. I've come to accept myself, realizing that I'm not so bad as I had always supposed myself to be. *Am I learning that my self-worth is not dependent on the approval of others, but instead is truly an "inside job"?*

Today I Pray

When I am feeling down and worthless, may my Higher Power and my friends in the group help me see that, although I was "fallen," I was not "cast down." However sick I might have been in my worst days, with all the self-esteem of an earthworm, may I know that I still had the power of choice. And I chose to do something about myself. May that good choice be the basis for my reactivated self-worth.

Today I Will Remember

I will not kick myself when I'm down.

Reflection for the Day

There's a world of difference between the idea of self-love and love of self. Self-love is a reflection of an inflated ego, around which—in our distorted view of our own self-importance—everything must revolve. *Self-love* is the breeding ground for hostility, arrogance, and a host of other character defects which blind us to any points of view but our own. *Love of self*, in contrast, is an appreciation of our dignity and value as human beings. Love of self is an expression of self-realization, from which springs humility. *Do I believe that I can love others best when I have gained love of self?*

Today I Pray

May God, who loves me, teach me to love myself. May I notice that the most arrogant and officious humans are not so completely sure of themselves, after all. Instead, they are apt to have a painfully low self-image, an insecurity which they cloak in pomp and princely trappings. May God show me that when I can like myself, I am duly crediting Him, since every living thing is a work of God.

Today I Will Remember

I will try to like myself.

Reflection for the Day

"Not all those who know their minds know their hearts as well," wrote La Rochefoucauld. The Program is of inestimable value for those of us, formerly addicted, who want to know ourselves and who are courageous enough to seek growth through self-examination and self-improvement. If I remain honest, open-minded, and willing, the Program will enable me to rid myself of my self-deceptive attitudes and character flaws that for so long prevented me from growing into the kind of person I want to be. *Do I try to help others understand the Program and Twelve Steps? Do I carry the message by example?*

Today I Pray

I ask God's blessing for the group, which has shown me so much about myself that I was not willing to face on my own. May I have the courage to be confronted and to confront, not only to be honest for honesty's sake—which may be reason enough—but to allow myself and the others in the group to grow in self-knowledge.

Today I Will Remember

We are mirrors of each other.

Reflection for the Day

"One's own self is well hidden from one's own self," a renowned philosopher once wrote. "Of all mines of treasure, one's own is the last to be dug up." The Twelve Steps have enabled me to unearth my "own self," the one that for so long was buried beneath my desperate need for approval from others. Thanks to the Program and my Higher Power, I've begun acquiring a true sense of self and a comfortable sense of confidence. No longer do I have to react chameleon-like, changing my coloration from one moment to the next fruitlessly trying to be all things to all people. *Do I strive, at all times, to be true to myself?*

Today I Pray

I pray that I may be honest with myself, and that I will continue—with the help of God and my friends—to try to get to know the real me. May I know that I cannot suddenly be a pulled-together, totally defined, completely consistent personality; it may take a while to develop into that personality, to work out my values and my priorities. May I know now that I have a good start on being who I want to be.

Today I Will Remember

I'm getting to be who I want to be.

Reflection for the Day

So many of us in the Program went through childhood—as well as part of our adult lives—emotionally shackled with the terrible burden called shyness. We found it difficult to walk into crowded rooms, to converse with even our friends, to make eye contact with *anyone*. The agonies we suffered! We learn in the Program that shyness is just another manifestation of self-centered fear, which is the root of all our character defects. Shyness, specifically, is fear of what others think or might think about us. To our enormous relief, our shyness gradually leaves us as we work the Program and interact with others. *Am I aware that I'm okay as long as I don't concentrate on me?*

Today I Pray

God, may I be grateful that I am getting over my shyness, after years of pulling back from people, squirming, blushing, blurting out all the "wrong things" or saying nothing at all—then reliving the agonies and imagining what I *should* have said and done. May I know that it has taken a full-blown addiction and a lot of caring people to convince me that I'm okay—and you're okay, he's okay and so is she.

Today I Will Remember

A cure for shyness is caring about somebody else.

Reflection for the Day

My addictions were like thieves in more ways than I can count. They robbed me not only of money, property, and other material things, but of dignity and self-respect, while my family and friends suffered right along with me. My addictions also robbed me of the ability to treat myself properly, as God would treat me. Today, in total contrast, I'm capable of true love of self—to the extent that I'm able to provide myself with more love than even I need. So I give that love away to other people in the Program, just as they have given their love to me. *Do I thank God for bringing me to a Program in which sick people are loved back to health?*

Today I Pray

Thanks be to God for a way of life which generates such love and caring that we in the Program can't help but learn to love ourselves. When I see that someone cares about me, I am more apt to be convinced that perhaps I am, after all, worth caring about. May I be conscious always of the love I am now able to give—and give it.

Today I Will Remember

Someone caring about me makes me feel worth caring about.

Reflection for the Day

From time to time when I see the slogan, *But for the Grace of God,* I remember how I used to mouth those words when I saw others whose addictions had brought them to what I considered a "hopeless and helpless" state. The slogan had long been a cop-out for me, reinforcing my denial of my own addiction by enabling me to point to others seemingly worse off than I. "If I ever get like that, I'll quit," was my oft-repeated refrain. Today, instead, *But for the Grace of God* has become my prayer of thankfulness, reminding me to be grateful to my Higher Power for my recovery, my life, and the *way* of life I've found in the Program. *Was anyone ever more "hopeless and helpless" than I?*

Today I Pray

May I know that but for the grace of God, I could be dead or insane by now, because there have been others who started on addictive paths when I did who are no longer here. May that same grace of God help those who are still caught in the downward spin, who are heading for disaster as sure as gravity.

Today I Will Remember

I have seen God's amazing grace.

Reflection for the Day

The Program's Fourth Step suggests that we make a fearless moral inventory of ourselves. For so many of us, especially newcomers, the task seems impossible. Each time we take pencil in hand and try to look inward, Pride says scoffingly, "You don't have to bother to look." And Fear cautions, "You'd better *not* look." We find eventually that pride and fear are mere wisps of smoke, the cloudy strands from which were woven the mythology of our old ideas. When we push pride and fear aside and finally make a fearless inventory, we experience relief and a new sense of confidence beyond description. *Have I made an inventory? Have I shared its rewards so as to encourage others?*

Today I Pray

May I not be stalled by my inhibitions when it comes to making a moral inventory of myself. May I not get to the Fourth Step and then screech to a stop because the task seems overwhelming. May I know that my inventory today, even though I try to make it "thorough" and honest, may not be as complete as it will be if I repeat it again, for the process of self-discovery goes on and on.

Today I Will Remember

Praise God for progress.

Reflection for the Day

"Pride, like a magnet, constantly points to one object, self; unlike the magnet, it has no attractive pole, but at all points repels," wrote *Colton*.

When the earliest members of the Program discovered just how spiritually prideful they could be, they admonished one another to avoid "instant sainthood." That old-time warning could be taken as an alibi to excuse us from doing our best, but it's really the Program's way of warning against "pride blindness" and the imaginary perfections we don't possess. *Am I beginning to understand the difference between pride and humility?*

Today I Pray

May God, who in His mercy has saved our lives, keep us from setting ourselves up as the saints and prophets of the Program. May we recognize the value of our experiences for others without getting smug about it. May we remember with humility and love the thousands of other "old hands" who are equally well-versed in its principles.

Today I Will Remember

I will avoid "instant sainthood."

Reflection for the Day

Virtually all of us suffered the defect of pride when we sought help through the Program, the Twelve Steps, and the fellowship of those who truly understood what we felt and where we had been. We learned about our shortcomings—and of pride in particular—and began to replace self-satisfaction with gratitude for the miracle of our recovery, gratitude for the privilege of working with others, and gratitude for God's gift, which enabled us to turn catastrophe into good fortune. *Have I begun to realize that "pride is to character as the attic to the house—the highest part, and generally the most empty..."?*

Today I Pray

God, please tell me if I am banging my shins on my own pride. Luckily for me, the Program has its own built-in check for flaws like this—the clear-eyed vision of the group, which sees in me what I sometimes cannot see myself. May I know that any kind of success has always gone straight to my head, and be watching for it as I begin to reconstruct my confidence.

Today I Will Remember

"Success" can be a setback.

Reflection for the Day

When I'm motivated by pride—by bondage of self—I become partly or even wholly blind to my liabilities and shortcomings. At that point, the last thing I need is comfort. Instead, I need an understanding friend in the Program—one who knows where I'm at—a friend who'll unhesitatingly chop a hole through the wall my ego has built so that the light of reason can once again shine through. *Do I take time to review my progress, to spot-check myself on a daily basis, and to promptly try to remedy my wrongs?*

Today I Pray

God I pray that the group—or just one friend—will be honest enough to see my slippery manifestations of pride and brave enough to tell me about them. My self-esteem was starved for so long, that with my first successes in the Program, it may swell to the gross proportions of self-satisfaction. May a view from outside myself give me a true picture of how I am handling the triumph of my sobriety—with humility or with pride.

Today I Will Remember

Self-esteem or self-satisfaction?

Reflection for the Day

If I'm to continue growing in the Program, I must literally "get wise to myself." I must remember that for most of my life I've been terribly self-deceived. The sin of pride has been at the root of most of my self-deception, usually masquerading under the guise of some virtue. I must work continually to uncover pride in all its subtle forms, lest it stop me in my tracks and push me backward once again to the brink of disaster. *When it comes to pride, do I believe, in Emerson's words, that "it is impossible for a man to be cheated by anyone but himself..."?*

Today I Pray

May I know that button-popping pride is inappropriate for me as a recovering addict. It hides my faults from me. It turns people off and gets in the way of my helping others. It halts my progress because it makes me think I've done enough self-searching and I'm cured. I pray to my Higher Power that I may be realistic enough to accept my success in the Program without giving in to pride.

Today I Will Remember

Pride halts progress.

Reflection for the Day

Those whom I most respect in the Program—and, in turn, those from whom I've learned the most—seem convinced that pride is, as one person put it, the "root-sin." In moral theology, pride is the first of the seven deadly sins. It is also considered the most serious, standing apart from the rest by virtue of its unique quality. Pride gets right into our spiritual victories. It insinuates itself into all our successes and accomplishments, even when we attribute them to God. *Do I struggle against pride by working the Tenth Step regularly, facing myself freshly and making things right where they've gone wrong?*

Today I Pray

May I be on guard constantly against the sneakiness of pride, which can creep into every achievement, every triumph, every reciprocated affection. May I know that whenever things are going well for me, my pride will be on the spot, ready to take credit. May I watch for it.

Today I Will Remember

Put pride in its place.

Reflection for the Day

The more self-searching we do, the more we realize how often we react negatively because our "pride has been hurt." Pride is at the root of most of my personal problems. When my pride is "hurt," for example, I almost invariably experience resentment and anger—sometimes to the point where I'm unable to talk or think rationally. When I'm in that sort of emotional swamp, I must remind myself that my pride—and nothing but *my pride*—has been injured. I have to pause and try to cool off until such time as I can evaluate the problem realistically. *When my pride is injured or threatened, will I pray for humility so that I can rise above myself?*

Today I Pray

May I know that if my pride is hurt, the rest of me may not be injured at all. May I know that my pride can take a battering and still come back stronger than ever for more. May I know that every time my pride takes a blow, it is liable to get more defensive, nastier, more unreasonable, more feisty. May I learn to keep my upstart pride in another place, where it will not be so easily hurt—or so willing to take credit.

Today I Will Remember

Humility is the only authority over pride.

Reflection for the Day

The Program's Twelve Steps comprise a body of *living* spiritual wisdom. To the degree that we continue to study the Steps and apply them to our daily lives, our knowledge and understanding expands without limitation. As we say in the Program, "It gets better...and better...and better." The Eleventh Step speaks of prayer and meditation, urging us to apply our minds quietly to the contemplation of spiritual truth. By its nature, the Eleventh Step illuminates for us the purpose and value of the other Steps. As we seek through prayer and meditation to improve our conscious contact with God, the remaining Steps become ever more useful in our new way of life. *Do I take the time each day to pray and meditate?*

Today I Pray

May I seek—as the Eleventh Step says—to know God better through prayer and meditation, talking to and listening for God. As my life becomes more full of the realities of earth—and the goodness thereof—may I always keep aside a time for communion with God. May this communion define my life and give it purpose.

Today I Will Remember

Take time out for God.

Reflection for the Day

We're taught in the Program that debate has no place in meditation. In a quiet place and time of our own choosing, we simply dwell on spiritual matters to the best of our capability, seeking only to experience and learn. We strive for a state of being which, hopefully, deepens our conscious contact with God. We pray not for things, but essentially for knowledge and power. *If you knew what God wanted you to do, you would be happy. You are doing what God wants you to do, so be happy.*

Today I Pray

May I find my own best way to God, my own best technique of meditation—whether I use the oriental mantra, substitute the name of Jesus Christ, or just allow the spirit of God, as I understand Him, to settle into me and give me peace. By whatever means I discover my God, may I learn to know Him well and feel His presence—not only at these quiet times, but in everything I do.

Today I Will Remember

Meditation is opening myself to the spirit of God.

Reflection for the Day

For many months after I came to the Program, I paid little attention to the practice of serious meditation and prayer. I felt that it might help me meet an emergency—such as a sudden craving to return to my old ways—but it remained among the lowest levels on my list of priorities. In those early days, I equated prayer and meditation with mystery and even hypocrisy. I've since found that prayer and meditation are more rewarding in their results than I could have ever imagined. For me today, the harvest is increasingly bountiful, and I continue to gain peace of mind and strength far beyond my human limitations. *Is my former pain being replaced by tranquility?*

Today I Pray

May I discover that prayer and meditation make up the central hall of my life's structure—the place where my thoughts collect and form into order. May I feel God's mystery there, and an overwhelming resource of energy.

Today I Will Remember

Fantasy is mine. Mystery is God's.

Reflection for the Day

There are no boundaries to meditation. It has neither width, depth, nor height, which means that it can always be further developed without limitation of any sort. Meditation is an individual matter; few of us meditate in the same way, and in that sense, it is truly a *personal* adventure. For all of us who practice meditation seriously, however, the purpose is the same: to improve our conscious contact with God. Despite its lack of specific dimensions and despite its intangibility, meditation is, in reality, the most intensely practical thing that we can do. One of its first rewards, for example, is emotional balance. What could be more practical than that? *Am I broadening and deepening the channel between myself and God?*

Today I Pray

As I seek God through daily prayer and meditation, may I find the peace that passes understanding, that balance that gives perspective to the whole of life. May I center myself in God.

Today I Will Remember

My balance comes from God.

Reflection for the Day

There are those in the Program who, at the beginning, shun meditation and prayer as they would avoid a pit filled with rattlesnakes. When they do finally take the first tentative and experimental step, however, and unexpected things begin to take place, they begin to feel different. Invariably, such tentative beginnings lead to true belief, to the extent that those who once belittled prayer and meditation become nothing less than walking advertisements for its rewards. We hear in the Program that "almost the only scoffers at prayer are those who never really tried it." *Is there an obstinate part of me that still scoffs?*

Today I Pray

May I learn, however irreverent I have been, that prayer is not to be mocked; I see the power of prayer effecting miracles around me, and I wonder. If I have refused to pray, may I look to see if pride is in my way—that old pride that insists on doing things on its own. Now that I have found a place for prayer in my life, may I reserve that place—religiously.

Today I Will Remember

Whoever learns to pray keeps on praying.

Reflection for the Day

My conscious contact with God depends entirely on me and on my *desire* for it. God's power is available for me to use at all times; whether I decide to use it or not is my choice. It has been said that "God is present in all His creatures, but all are not equally aware of His presence." I'll try to remind myself every day of how much depends on my awareness of God's influence in my life. And I'll try to accept His help in everything I do. *Will I remember that God knows how to help me, that He can help me, and that He wants to help me?*

Today I Pray

May I be aware always that God's power and peace are a bottomless well within me. I can draw bucket after bucket from it to refresh and purify my life. All I need to supply are the buckets and the rope. The water is mine—free, fresh, healing, and unpolluted.

Today I Will Remember

The well is God's; I bring the buckets.

Reflection for the Day

As time passes, daily communion with God is becoming as essential to me as breathing in and out. I don't need a special place to pray, because God always hears my call. I don't need special words with which to pray, because God already knows my thoughts and my needs. I have only to turn my attention to God, aware that His attention is always turned to me. *Do I know that only good can come to me if I trust God completely?*

Today I Pray

May my communion with God become a regular part of my life, as natural as a heartbeat. May I find, as I grow accustomed to the attitude of prayer, that it becomes less important to find a corner of a room, a bedside, a church pew, or even a special time of day, for prayer. May my thoughts turn to God automatically and often, whenever there is a lull in my day or a need for direction.

Today I Will Remember

Let prayer become a habit.

Reflection for the Day

When I first came to the Program, I thought that humility was just another word for weakness. But I gradually learned that there's nothing incompatible between humility and intellect, just as long as I place humility first. As soon as I began to do that, I was told, I would receive the gift of faith—a faith which would work for me as it has worked and continues to work for countless others who have been freed of their addictions and have found a new way of life in the Program. *Have I come to believe, in the words of Heine, that "the actions of men are like the index of a book; they point out what is most remarkable in them..."?*

Today I Pray

May I never let my intelligence be an excuse for lack of humility. It is so easy, if I consider myself reasonably bright and capable of making decisions and handling my own affairs, to look down upon humility as a property of those less intelligent. May I remember that intelligence and humility are both God-given.

Today I Will Remember

If I have no humility, I have no intelligence.

I've always been drawn to people who are understated rather than braggarts

Reflection for the Day

What, exactly, is humility? Does it mean that we are to be submissive, accepting everything that comes our way, no matter how humiliating? Does it mean surrender to ugliness and a destructive way of life? On the contrary. The basic ingredient of all humility is simply a desire to seek and do God's will. *Am I coming to understand that an attitude of true humility confers dignity and grace on me, strengthening me to take intelligent spiritual action in solving my problems?*

Today I Pray

May I discover that humility is not bowing and scraping, kowtowing, or letting people walk all over me—all of which have built-in expectations of some sort of personal reward, like approval or sympathy. Real humility is awareness of the vast love and unending might of God. It is the perspective that tells me how I, as a human being, relate to that Divine Power.

Today I Will Remember

Humility is awareness of God.

Reflection for the Day

There are few "absolutes" in the Program's Twelve Steps. We're free to start at any point we can, or will. God, as we understand Him, may be defined as simply a "Power greater"; for many of us in the Program, the group itself was the first "Power greater." And this acknowledgment is relatively easy to make if a newcomer knows that most of the members are sober and otherwise chemically free and he or she isn't. This admission is the beginning of humility. Perhaps for the first time, the newcomer is at least willing to disclaim that he himself—or she herself—is God. *Is my behavior more convincing to newcomers than my words?*

Today I Pray

May I define and discover my own Higher Power. As that definition becomes clearer and closer to me, may I remember not to insist that my interpretation is right. For each must find his or her own Higher Power. If a newcomer is feeling godless and alone, the power of the group may be enough for now. May I never discredit the power of the group.

Today I Will Remember

Group power can be a Higher Power.

Reflection for the Day

We hear it said that all progress in the Program can be boiled down and measured by just two words: humility and responsibility. It's also said that our entire spiritual development can be precisely measured by our degree of adherence to those standards. As AA co-founder Bill W. once put it, "Ever deepening humility, accompanied by an ever greater willingness to accept and to act upon clear-cut obligations—these are truly our touchstones for all growth in the life of the spirit." *Am I responsible?*

Today I Pray

I pray that of all the good words and catch phrases and wisps of inspiration that come to me, I will remember these two above all: humility and responsibility. These may be the hardest to come by—humility because it means shooing away my pride, responsibility because I am in the habit of using my addiction as a thin excuse for getting out of obligations. I pray that I may break these old patterns.

Today I Will Remember

First humility, then responsibility.

Reflection for the Day

First search for a little humility, my sponsor urged me. If you don't, he said, you're greatly increasing the risk of going out there again. After a while, in spite of my lifelong rebelliousness, I took his advice; I began to try to practice humility, simply because I believed it was the right thing to do. Hopefully, the day will come when most of my rebelliousness will be but a memory, and then I'll practice humility because I deeply want it as a way of life. *Can I try today, to leave my self behind and to seek the humility of self-forgetfulness?*

Today I Pray

Since I—like so many chemically or otherwise dependent people—am a rebel, may I know that I will need to practice humility. May I recognize that humility does not come easily to a rebellious nature, whether I am out-and-out defiant, dug-in negative, or, more subtly, determined in a roundabout way to change everything else but myself. I pray that by practicing humility it will become instinctive for me.

Today I Will Remember

Get the humble habit.

Reflection for the Day

As a newcomer, I was told that my admission of my powerlessness over alcohol was my first step toward freedom from its deadly grip; I soon came to realize the truth of that fact. In that regard, surrender was a dire necessity. But for me that was only a small beginning toward acquiring humility. I've learned in the Program that to be willing to work for humility—as something to be desired for itself—takes most of us a long, long time. *Do I realize that a whole lifetime geared to self-centeredness can't be shifted into reverse in a split second?*

Today I Pray

May I search for my own humility as a quality that I must cultivate to survive, not just an admission that I am powerless over my compulsive behavior. Step One is just that—step one in the direction of acquiring an attitude of humility. May I be realistic enough to know that this may take half a lifetime.

Today I Will Remember

Pride blew it; let humility have a chance.

Reflection for the Day

We sometimes hear humility defined as the state of being "teachable." In that sense, most of us in the Program who are able to stay free of active addiction have acquired at least a smattering of humility, or we never would have learned to stay away from the first drink, the first tranquilizer, the first "side bet," and similar destructive acts for those of us who are powerless over our respective addictions. *Do I see increasing humility as a pathway to continuing improvement?*

Today I Pray

Now that I have made a start at developing humility, may I keep it up. May I open myself to the will of God and the suggestions of my friends in the group. May I remain teachable, confrontable, receptive, and conscious that I must stay that way in order to be healthy.

Today I Will Remember

To remain confrontable.

Reflection for the Day

Many of us in the Program stubbornly cling to false ideas and positions simply because we fear we'd be left defenseless if we admitted having been wrong. The thought of "backing down" still seems distasteful to some of us. But we come to learn that our self-esteem soars when we're able to push pride into the background and truly face the facts. Chances are that people with true humility have more genuine self-esteem than those of us who are repeatedly victimized by pride. *Does pride deviously keep me from thorough and continuing attention to the Tenth Step?*

Today I Pray

May pride stay out of my way, now that I've found a road to follow. May I avoid that familiar, destructive cycle of pride—the ego that balloons up out of all proportion and then deflates with a fizzle. May I learn the value of "backing down."

Today I Will Remember

Pride is the arch-enemy of self-esteem.

NOVEMBER 18

Reflection for the Day

"Nothing is enough to the man for whom enough is too little," wrote the Greek philosopher Epicurus. Now that we're free from addiction, rebuilding our self-respect and winning back the esteem of family and friends, we have to avoid becoming smug about our new-found success. For most of us, success has always been a heady brew; even in our new life, it's still possible to fall into the dangerous trap of "big-shot-itis." As insurance, we ought to remember that we're free today only by the grace of God. *Will I remember that any success I may be having is far more His success than mine?* So is any failure

Today I Pray

May I keep a constant string-on-the-finger reminder that I have found freedom through the grace of God—just so I don't let my pride try to convince me I did it all myself. May I learn to cope with success by ascribing it to a Higher Power, not to my own questionable superiority.

Today I Will Remember

Learn to deal with success.

Reflection for the Day

I no longer argue with people who believe that satisfaction of our natural desires is the primary purpose of life. It's not our business in the Program to knock material achievement. When we stop and think about it, in fact, no group of people ever made a worse mess of trying to live by that "la dolce vita" formula than we did. We always insisted on more than our share—in all areas. And even when we seemed to be succeeding, we fueled our addictions so that we could dream of still greater successes. *Am I learning that material satisfactions are simply by-products and not the chief aim of life? Am I gaining the perspective to see that character-building and spiritual values must come first?*

Today I Pray

May I recognize that I never did handle excesses very well, based on my past experience. I have been apt to "want more" of whatever it is I have—love, money, property, things, chemicals, foods, winnings. May the Program teach me that I must concentrate on my spiritual, rather than my material bounty.

Today I Will Remember

It's okay to be spiritually greedy.

Reflection for the Day

I've come to measure success in a whole new way. My success today isn't limited by social or economic benchmarks. Success is mine today, no matter what the undertaking, when I tap the power of God within me and allow myself to be an open channel for the expression of His good. The spirit of success works through me as increased vision and understanding, as creative ideas and useful service—as efficient use of my time and energy, and as cooperative effort with others. *Will I try to keep my mind centered in the realization that within me is the God-implanted power to succeed?*

Today I Pray

May I develop a new concept of success, based on measurements of the good qualities which come from God's treasure-filled bank of good. To draw from that bank, all I have to do is look within myself. May I know that God's riches are the only kind that are fully insurable, because they are infinite. May I look in God's bank for my security.

Today I Will Remember

Spiritual "success" is my security.

Reflection for the Day

Adversity introduces man to himself, a poet once said. For me, the same is true of even *imagined* adversity. If I expect another person to react in a certain way in a given situation—and he or she fails to meet my expectation—well, then I hardly have the right to be disappointed or angry. Yet I occasionally still experience feelings of frustration when people don't act or react as I think they should. Through such imagined—or, better yet, *self-inflicted*—adversity, I come face to face again with my old self, the one who wanted to run the whole show. *Is it finally time for me to stop expecting and to start accepting?*

Today I Pray

May I stop putting words in people's mouths, programming them—in my own mind—to react as I expect them to. Expectations have fooled me before: I expected unbounded love and protection from those close to me, perfection from myself, undivided attention from casual acquaintances. On the adverse side, I expected failure from myself, and rejection from others. May I stop borrowing trouble—or triumph either—from the future.

Today I Will Remember

Accept. Don't expect.

Reflection for the Day

"We succeed in enterprises which demand the positive qualities we possess," wrote de Tocqueville, "but we excel in those which can also make use of our defects." We learn in the Program that our defects do have value—to the extent that we use them as the starting point for change and the pathway to better things. Fear can be a stepping stone to prudence, for example, as well as to respect for others. Fear can also help us turn away from hate and toward understanding. In the same way, pride can lead us toward the road of humility. *Am I aware of my direction today? Do I care where I'm going?*

Today I Pray

I pray that my Higher Power will show me how to use my defects in a positive way, because nothing—not even fear or selfishness or greed—is all bad. May I trust that every quality that leads me into trouble has a reverse side that can lead me out. Pride, for instance, can't puff itself up unduly without bursting and demonstrating that it is, in essence, only hot air. May I learn from my weaknesses.

Today I Will Remember

Good news out of bad.

Reflection for the Day

Before I came to the Program, I was like an actor who insisted on writing the script, producing, directing, and, in short, running the whole show. I had to do it *my* way, forever trying to arrange and re-arrange the lights, lines, sets, and, most of all, the other players' performances. If only my arrangements would stay put, and people would behave as I wished, the show would be fantastic. My self-delusion led me to believe that if *they* all would just shape up, everything would be fine. Of course, it never worked out that way. *Isn't it amazing how others seem to be "shaping up" now that I've stopped trying to manage everything and everybody?*

Today I Pray

May I talk myself out of that old urge to control everything and everybody. Time was, if I couldn't manage directly, I would do it indirectly, through manipulation, secret conferences, and asides. May I know that if I am the one who is always pulling the strings on the marionettes, then I am also the one who feels the frustration when they collapse or slip off the stage.

Today I Will Remember

I can only "shape up" myself.

Reflection for the Day

Although we came into the Program to deal with a specific problem, we soon became aware that we would find not only freedom from addiction, but freedom to live in the real world without fear and frustration. We learned that the solutions are within ourselves. With the help of my Higher Power, I can enrich my life with comfort, enjoyment, and deep-down serenity. *Am I changing from my own worst enemy to my own best friend?*

Today I Pray

May I praise my Higher Power for my freedoms—from addiction, from spiritual bankruptcy, from loneliness, from fear, from the seesaw of pride, from despair, from delusions, from shallowness, from doom. I give thanks for the way of life that has given me these freedoms and replaces the empty spaces with extra goodness and peace of mind.

Today I Will Remember

To give thanks for *all* my freedoms.

Reflection for the Day

"What you have may seem small; you desire so much more. See children thrusting their hands into a narrow necked jar, striving to pull out the sweets. If they fill the hand, they cannot pull it out and then they fall to tears. When they let go a few, they can draw out the rest. You, too, let your desire go; covet not too much...", wrote *Epictetus*.

Let me expect not too much of anyone, particularly myself. Let me learn to settle for less than I wish were possible, and be willing to accept it and appreciate it. *Do I accept gratefully and graciously the good that has already come to me in the Program?*

Today I Pray

May I search my soul for those little hankerings of want which may keep me from delighting in all that I have. If I can just teach myself not to want too much, not to expect too much, then when those expectations are not satisfied, I will not be let down. May I accept with grace what the grace of God has provided.

Today I Will Remember

I, alone, can grant myself the "freedom from want."

Reflection for the Day

During our first days in the Program we got rid of alcohol and pills. We had to get rid of our chemicals, for we knew they surely would have killed us. We got rid of the addictive substances, but we couldn't get rid of our addictions until we took further action. So we also had to learn to toss self-pity, self-justification, self-righteousness, and self-will straight out the window. We had to get off the rickety ladder that supposedly led to money, property, and prestige. And we had to take personal responsibility. To gain enough humility and self-respect to stay alive at all, we had to give up our most valued possessions—our ambition and our pride. *Am I well rid of the weights and chains that once bound me?*

Today I Pray

May I give credit to my Higher Power not only for removing my addiction, but for teaching me to remove my old demanding, pushy "self" from all my spiritual and earthly relationships. For all the things I have learned and unlearned, for my own faith and for the grace of God, I am fully and heartily thankful.

Today I Will Remember

Gratitude for the grace of God.

Reflection for the Day

The Program shows us how to transform the pipe-dreams of our pasts into reality and true sense of purpose, together with a growing consciousness of the power of God in our lives. It's all right to keep our heads in the clouds with Him, we're taught, but our feet should remain firmly planted here on earth. Here's where other people are; here's where our work must be accomplished. *Do I see anything incompatible between spirituality and a useful life in the here and now?*

Today I Pray

May my new "reality" include not only the nuts and bolts and pots and pans of daily living, but also my spiritual reality, my growing knowledge of the presence of God. May this new reality have room, too, for my dreams—not the drug-induced, mind-drifting fantasies of the past or the remnants of my delusions, but the products of a healthy imagination. May I respect these dreams, anchor them in earth's possibilities, and turn them into useful creativity.

Today I Will Remember

Heaven has a place in the here and now.

Reflection for the Day

Our faith in God's power—at work in us and in our lives—doesn't relieve us of responsibility. Instead, our faith strengthens our efforts, makes us confident and assured, and enables us to act decisively and wisely. We're no longer afraid to make decisions; we're not afraid to take the steps that seem called for in the proper handling of given situations. *Do I believe that God is at work beyond my human efforts, and that my faith and trust in Him will bring forth results far exceeding my expectations?*

Today I Pray

May my trust in my Higher Power never falter. May my faith in that Power continue to shore up my optimism, my confidence, my belief in my own decision making. May I never shut my eyes to the wonder of God's work or discount the wisdom of His solutions.

Today I Will Remember

Our hope in ages past, our help for years to come.

Reflection for the Day

Contrary to what some people think, our slogan, *Let Go and Let God,* isn't an expression of apathy, an attitude of defeatism, or an unwillingness to accept responsibility. Those who turn their backs on their problems are not "letting go and letting God," but, instead, are abandoning their commitment to act on God's inspiration and guidance. They neither ask for nor expect help; they want God to do it *all. In seeking God's guidance, do I realize that the ultimate responsibility is mine?*

Today I Pray

May I not allow myself to be lazy just because I think God is going to do everything anyway. (Such apathy reminds me of my old powerless self, the one that moaned that the world was going up in smoke, civilization was going down the drain, and there wasn't a thing I could do about it.) Neither may I use "letting God" do it as an excuse for shrugging off my problems without even trying. May God be my inspiration; may I be an instrument of God.

Today I Will Remember

God guides those who help themselves.

Reflection for the Day

If you're a negative thinker and are not yet ready to do an about-face, here are some guidelines that can keep you miserable for just as long as you wish to remain so. First, don't go to meetings of the Program, especially discussion groups. If you somehow find yourself at a meeting, keep your mouth shut, your hands in your pockets, and your mind closed. Don't try to solve any of your problems, never laugh at yourself, and don't trust the other people in the Program. Above all, under no conditions should you try to live in the Now. *Am I aware that negative thinking means taking myself deadly serious at all times, leaving no time for laughter—and for living?*

Today I Pray

If I am feeling negative, may I check myself in the mirror that is the group for any symptoms of a closed mind: tight lips, forced smile, set jaw, straight-ahead glance—and no glimmer of humor. God, grant me the ability to laugh at myself—often—for I need that laughter to cope with the everyday commotion of living.

Today I Will Remember

To laugh at myself.

DECEMBER 1

Reflection for the Day

It has truly been said that "We become what we do." It's emphasized to us over and over in the Program that our thoughts and actions toward others color and shape our spiritual lives. Words and acts of kindness, generosity, thoughtfulness, and forgiveness serve to strengthen those qualities within us that heighten our consciousness of God's love. *In asking God to direct and guide my life, am I also asking love to take over and lead me where it will?*

Today I Pray

May I make a resolute attempt at acting out the way I want to be—loving, forgiving, kind, thoughtful. May I be aware that each small, attentive act carries with it an echo of God's all-caring. For God so loved the world...may we make His love our example.

Today I Will Remember

We become what we do.

Reflection for the Day

Once at a meeting held in a church, I saw a stained glass window on which was written, "God Is Love." For some reason, my mind transposed the words into "Love is God." Either way is correct and true, I realized, looking about me and becoming even more conscious of the spirit of love and Power in the small meeting room. I'll continue to seek out that love and Power, following the Program as if my life depended upon it—as indeed it does. *Does life to me today mean living—in the active sense—joyously and comfortably?*

Today I Pray

May I feel the spirit of love that gives our prayers their energy. May I feel the oneness in this room, the concentration of love that gives the group its power. May I feel the exemplary love of a Higher Power, which our love echoes.

Today I Will Remember

Love is God.

Reflection for the Day

Our ancient enemy, self-will, wears a mask, confronting me with this sort of rationalization: "Why do I have to lean on God? Hasn't He already given me the intelligence to think for myself?" I have to pause when such thoughts creep into my mind, remembering that I've never really been able to bring about the results I wanted simply by relying on my own devices. I'm not self-sufficient, nor do I know all the answers; bitter experience alone teaches me that. *Do I know that I need God's guidance? Am I willing to accept it?*

Today I Pray

I pray that, as I become stronger in my conviction and in my sobriety, I will not begin to shrug off my dependence on a Higher Power. May I continue to pray for guidance, even when things seem to be going along smoothly. May I know that I need my Higher Power as much in times of triumph as in times of trauma.

Today I Will Remember

Self-sufficiency is a godless myth.

Reflection for the Day

Most of us in the Program are far more comfortable with the determination that we won't take the first drink *today*, than we are with the "vow" that we'll *never drink again*. Saying "I intend never to drink again" is quite different from saying "I'll never drink again." The last statement is far too reflective of self-will; it doesn't leave much room for the idea that God will remove our obsession to drink if we practice the Program's Twelve Steps one day at a time. *Will I continue to fight against complacency, realizing that I'll always be just one drink away from disaster?*

Today I Pray

"Never again" demands too binding a commitment, even for the strongest among us. Our past lives were full of "never agains" and "won't evers," promises that were broken before the next dawn. May I, for now, set my sights on just one straight, sober day at a time.

Today I Will Remember

Never say "never again."

Reflection for the Day

"It is of low benefit to give me something. It is of high benefit to enable me to do something for myself," wrote *Emerson*.

I've been taught in the Program that I begin to use my will properly when I try to make it conform with God's will. In the past, most of my problems resulted from the *improper* use of will power. I'd always tried to use it, in sledgehammer fashion, as a way of solving my problems or changing the conditions of my life. *Do I see that a primary purpose of the Twelve Steps is to help me channel my will into agreement with God's intentions for me?*

Today I Pray

May I direct my will power into a channel where it can pick up the will of God. May I no longer use my will power—which has not proved mighty in the past—as willfulness. May I think of my will only as an extension of God's will, listening always for direction.

Today I Will Remember

To use my will power as willingness, not willfulness.

Reflection for the Day

When I finally convince myself to let go of a problem that's been tearing me apart—when I take the action to set aside my will and let God handle the problem—my torment subsides immediately. If I continue to stay out of my own way, then solutions begin to unfold and reveal themselves. More and more, I'm coming to accept the limitations of my human understanding and power. More and more, I'm learning to let go and trust my Higher Power for the answers and the help. *Do I keep in the forefront of my mind the fact that only God is all-wise and all-powerful?*

Today I Pray

If I come across a stumbling-block, may I learn to step out of the way and let God remove it. May I realize my human limitations at problem-solving, since I can never begin to predict God's solutions until I see them happening. May I know that whatever answer I come to, God may have a better one.

Today I Will Remember

God has a better answer.

Reflection for the Day

As long as I stubbornly hang on to the conviction that I can live solely by my individual strength and intelligence, a working faith in my Higher Power is impossible. This is true, no matter how strongly I believe that God exists. My religious beliefs—no matter how sincere—will remain forever lifeless if I continue trying to play God myself. What it comes down to, we find, is that, as long as we place self-reliance first, true reliance upon a Higher Power is out of the question. *How strong is my desire to seek and do God's will?*

Today I Pray

I pray that I may not place my self-reliance above reliance on God. May I know that there is no conflict between taking responsibility for my own actions, which I have been taught is the essence of maturity, and looking to God for guidance. May I remember that if I stick to the "do it myself" rule, it is like refusing to ask for a road map from a tourist information bureau —and wandering around forever lost.

Today I Will Remember

Maturity is knowing where to go for help.

Reflection for the Day

We often see people in the Program—devoutly and with seeming sincerity—ask for God's guidance on matters ranging from major crises to such insignificant things as what to serve at a dinner party. Though they may be well-intentioned, such people tend to force their wills into all sorts of situations—with the comfortable assurance that they're following God's specific directions. In reality, this sort of prayer is nothing more than a self-serving demand of God for "replies"; it has little to do with the Program's suggested Eleventh Step. *Do I strive regularly to study each of the Steps, and to practice them in all my affairs?*

Today I Pray

May I not make the common mistake of listing my own solutions for God and then asking for a stamp of Divine approval. May I catch myself if I am not really opening my mind to God's guidance, but merely laying out my own answers with a "what do You think of these?" attitude.

Today I Will Remember

Am I looking for God's rubber stamp?

Reflection for the Day

"Difficulties are God's errands, and when we are sent upon them, we should esteem it a proof of God's confidence," wrote *Beecher*.

I've come to realize that my past troubles were really of my own making. Although I hardly thought so at the time, I was a primary example of what the Program calls "self-will run riot." Today I'll accept my difficulties as signposts to growth and as evidence of God's confidence in me. *Do I believe that God will never give me more than I can handle?*

Today I Pray

May I believe strongly that God has confidence in me to handle my troubles, that the difficulties I must face are in direct proportion to my strength and ability to bear up and keep a cool head in a crisis. May I also understand that it is my faith in God which keeps me from crumbling.

Today I Will Remember

God has faith in me, because I have faith in God.

Reflection for the Day

Have I ever stopped to think that the impulse to "blow off steam" and say something unkind or even vicious will, if followed through, hurt me far more seriously than the person to whom the insult is directed? I must try constantly to quiet my mind before I act with impatience or hostility, for my mind can be—in that very real way —an enemy as great as any I've ever known. *Will I look before I leap, think before I speak—and try to avoid self-will to the greatest extent possible?*

Today I Pray

May I remember that my blow-ups and explosions, when they are torrents of accusations or insults, hurt me just as much as the other person. May I try not to let my anger get to the blow-up stage, simply by recognizing it as I go along and stating it as a fact.

Today I Will Remember

Keep a loose lid on the teapot.

Reflection for the Day

Before I came to the Program—in fact, before I knew of the Program's existence—I drifted from crisis to crisis. Occasionally, I tried to use my will to chart a new course; however, like a rudderless ship, I inevitably foundered once again on the rocks of my own despair. Today, in contrast, I receive guidance from my Higher Power. Sometimes, the only answer is a sense of peace or an assurance that all is well. *Even though there may be a time of waiting before I see results, or before any direct guidance comes, will I try to remain confident that things are working out in ways that will be for the greatest good of everyone concerned?*

Today I Pray

May I not expect instant, verbal communication with my Higher Power, like directions on a stamped, self-addressed post-card. May I have patience, and listen, and sense that God is present. May I accept my new feeling of radiant warmth and serenity as God's way of assuring me that I am, finally, making some good choices.

Today I Will Remember

Patience: God's message will come.

Reflection for the Day

These days, if I go through an experience that is *challenging* new and demanding, I can do so in a spirit of confidence and trust. Thanks to the Program and Twelve Steps, I've come to know that God is with me in all places and in all endeavors. His Spirit is in me as well as in the people around me. As a result, I feel comfortable even in new situations and at home even among strangers. *Will I continue to flow along and grow along with the Program, trusting in the power and love of God at work in me and in my life?*

Today I Pray

May God's comfort be with me in all situations, familiar or new. May He rebuild the sagging bridge of my confidence. May I acknowledge God in me and in others around me. May that mutual identity in God help me communicate with people on a plane of honesty. If I can learn to trust God, I can learn to trust the ones who share this earth with me.

Today I Will Remember

God teaches me how to trust.

Reflection for the Day

A friend in the Program told me of a favorite hymn from her childhood: "Open my eyes that I may see glimpses of truth Thou hast for me." In actuality, that is what the Program has done for me—it has opened my eyes so that I have come to see the true nature of my addiction, as well as the true nature of the joyous life that can be mine if I practice the principles embodied in the Program's Twelve Steps to recovery. *Through prayer and meditation, am I also improving my inner vision, so that I can better see God's love and power working in me and through me?*

Today I Pray

glimpse

May each glint of truth that I catch sight of as I work the Steps begin to take on the steadier shine of a fixed star. May I know that these stars are all that I need to chart my course and navigate safely. May I no longer feel the frantic need to put in to every unknown port along the way in search of direction. These stars are always mine to steer by.

Today I Will Remember

Find the fixed stars and fix on them.

Reflection for the Day

Some of us in the Program are inclined to make the mistake of thinking that the few moments we spend in prayer and meditation—in "talking with God"—are all that count. The truth is that the attitude we maintain throughout the entire day is just as important. If we place ourselves in God's hands in the morning, and throughout the day hold ourselves ready to accept His will as it is made known through the events of our daily life, our attitude of acceptance becomes a *constant* prayer. *Can I try to cultivate an attitude of total acceptance each day?*

Today I Pray

May I maintain contact with my Higher Power all through my day, not just check in for a prayer now and then. May my communion with God never become merely a casual aside. May I come to know that every time I do something that is in accord with God's will I am living a prayer.

Today I Will Remember

Prayer is an attitude.

Reflection for the Day

Some people are such worriers that they feel sorry about the fact that they have nothing to worry about. Newcomers in the Program sometimes feel, for example, "This is much too good to last." Most of us, however, have plenty of real things to worry about—old standbys like money, health, death, and taxes, to name just a few. But the Program tells us that the proven antidote to worry and fear is confidence—confidence not in ourselves, but in our Higher Power. *Will I continue to believe that God can and will avert the calamity that I spend my days and nights dreading? Will I believe that if calamity does strike, God will enable me to see it through?*

Today I Pray

May I realize that the worry habit—worry that grows out of broader, often unlabeled fears—will take more than time to conquer. Like many dependent people, I have lived with worry so long that it has become my constant, floor-pacing companion. May my Higher Power teach me that making a chum out of worry is a waste of my energy and fritters away my constructive hours.

Today I Will Remember

Kick the worry habit.

Reflection for the Day

Sometimes, on those bad days we all have from time to time, it almost seems that God doesn't want us to be happy here on earth and, for those of us who believe in an afterlife, that He demands pain and suffering in this life as the price of happiness in the next. The Program teaches me that just the opposite is the case. God wants me to be happy right here on earth—right now. When I allow Him to, He will even point out the way. *Do I sometimes stubbornly refuse to look where God is pointing?*

Today I Pray

I pray that I am not playing the perennial sufferer, dragging around in the boots of tragedy and acting as if suffering is the only ticket to heaven. May I look around, at the goodness and greenery of earth, which is testimony enough that our life here is meant to be more than just one pitfall after another. May no misconception of God as a master trapper, waiting in every thicket to snare us, distort my relationship with a loving, forgiving Higher Power.

Today I Will Remember

There is more to life than suffering.

DECEMBER 17

Reflection for the Day

More and more these days, as I progress in my recovery, I seem to do a lot of *listening*—quietly waiting to hear God's unmistakable voice within me. Prayer is becoming a two-way street—of seeking and listening, of searching and finding. A favorite bit of Scripture for me is, "Be still and know that I am God." *Do I pay quiet and loving attention to Him, evermore confident of an enlightened knowledge of His will for me?*

Today I Pray

As I seek to know my Higher Power, may I learn the best ways—for me—to reach and hear Him. May I begin to *feel* prayer, not just listen to the sound of my own verbalizing. May I feel the sharp outlines of my humanness fading as His Godliness becomes a part of me. May I feel that I am one with Him.

Today I will Remember

Feel the stillness of God.

Reflection for the Day

I'm learning—all too slowly, at times—that when I give up the losing battle of trying to run my life in my own way, I gain abiding peace and deep serenity. For many of us, that learning process is a painfully slow one. Eventually, however, I understand that there are only two wills in the world, my will and God's. Whatever is within my direct control is my will, whatever is beyond my direct control is His will. So I try to accept that which is beyond my control as God's will for me. *Am I beginning to realize that by surrendering my will to the Divine Will, I am for the first time living without turmoil and without anxiety?*

Today I Pray

May I hope that my will can be congruent with the all-encompassing will of God. I pray that I will know immediately if my will is in a useless tug of war with His Divine Will. May I trust God now to guide my will according to His Master Plan—and to make His purpose mine.

Today I Will Remember

Achievement comes when my will is in harmony with God's.

Reflection for the Day

The Program teaches me to work for progress, not perfection. That simple admonition gives me great comfort, for it represents a primary way in which my life today is so different from what it used to be. In my former life, *perfection*—for all its impossibility—was so often my number one goal. Today I can believe that if I sometimes fail, *I'm* not a failure—and if I sometimes make mistakes, *I'm* not a mistake. And I can apply those same beliefs to the Program's Twelve Steps as well as to my entire life. *Do I believe that only Step One can be practiced with perfection, and that the remaining Steps represent perfect ideals?*

Today I Pray

God, teach me to abandon my erstwhile goal of superhuman perfection in everything I did or said. I know now that I was actually bent on failure, because I could never attain those impossible heights I had established for myself. Now that I understand this pattern, may I no longer program my own failures.

Today I Will Remember

I may strive to be a super person, but not a superperson.

Reflection for the Day

When we compulsively strive for perfection, we invariably injure ourselves. For one thing, we end up creating big problems from little ones. For another, we become frustrated and filled with despair when we're unable to meet the impossible goals we've set for ourselves. And finally, we decrease our capability to deal with life and reality as they are. *Can I learn to yield a little, here and there? Can I apply myself with a quiet mind only to what is possible and attainable?*

Today I Pray

May I see that striving for an impossible accomplishment provides me with an ever-ready excuse for not making it. It is also an indication of my loss of reality sense, which ought to involve knowing what I can do and then doing it. With the help of the group and my Higher Power, may I learn to set "reasonable goals." These may seem ridiculously small to me, after years of thinking big. But, by breaking down my projects into several smaller ones, may I find that I actually can accomplish some high goals.

Today I Will Remember

Break down large goals into smaller ones.

Reflection for the Day

Each of us in the Program can, in our own time and own way, reach the triumphant spiritual awakening that is described in the Twelfth Step. The spiritual awakening is a deep-down knowledge that we are no longer alone and helpless. It's also a deep-down awareness that we've learned certain truths which we cannot transmit to others so that perhaps they, too, can be helped. *Am I keeping myself in constant readiness for the spiritual awakening which is certain to come to me as I practice the Steps and surrender my will to God's will?*

Today I Pray

May I be steady, not expecting that my spiritual awakening will startle me like an alarm clock into sudden awareness of a Higher Power. It may settle on me so quietly that I may not recognize precisely when my moment of awareness comes. The clue may come in my desire to Twelfth-Step others. May I realize, then, that I have accepted the principles of the Program and am at home with the spiritual transformation I feel in myself.

Today I Will Remember

My spiritual awakening is my first private moment with God.

Reflection for the Day

Through our own experiences and the experiences of others in the Program, we see that a spiritual awakening is in reality a gift—a gift which in essence is a new state of consciousness and being. It means that I'm now on a road which really leads somewhere; it means that life is really worth living, rather than something to be endured. It means that I have been transformed in the sense that I have undergone a basic personality change—and that I possess a source of strength which I had so long denied myself. *Do I believe that none come too soon to the Program, and that none return too late?*

Today I Pray

I pray that I may attain that state of consciousness which transcends my everyday reality—but is also a part of it. May I no longer question the existence of God because I have touched His Being. For us who are recovering from addictions, the words reborn in the Spirit have a special, precious meaning. May I be wholly grateful to a Higher Power for leading me to a spiritual rebirth.

Today I Will Remember

Renaissance through my Higher Power.

Reflection for the Day

How can I tell if I have had a spiritual awakening? For many of us in the Program, a spiritual awakening manifests itself in simple, rather than complicated, evidences: emotional maturity; an end to constant and soul churning resentments; the ability to love and be loved in return; the belief, even without understanding, that something lets the sun rise and set, brings forth and ends life, and gives joy to human hearts. *Am I now able to do, feel, and believe that which I could not previously do through my own unaided strength and resources alone?*

Today I Pray

May my spiritual confidence begin to spread over my attitudes towards others, especially during holiday times, when anticipations and anxieties are high. As an addictive person, I have not handled holidays well—greeting those who gather at home, missing those who are not here. I pray for serenity to cope with the holiday brew of emotions.

Today I Will Remember

Spirit without "spirits." Cheer without "cheer."

Reflection for the Day

We came to the Program as supplicants, literally at the ends of our ropes. Sooner or later, by practicing the principles of the Twelve Steps, we discover within ourselves a very precious thing. We uncover something with which we can be comfortable in all places and situations. We gain strength and grow with the help of God as we understand Him, with the fellowship of the Program, and by applying the Twelve Steps to our lives. *Can anyone take my new life from me?*

Today I Pray

May my prayers of desperate supplication, which I brought to my God as a newcomer to the Program, change to a peaceful surrender to the will of God. Now that I have seen what can be done through the endless might of a Higher Power, may my gift to others be that strong conviction. I pray that those I love will have the faith to find their own spiritual experiences and the blessings of peace.

Today I Will Remember

Peace—inner and outer—is God's greatest blessing.

Reflection for the Day

Today is a special day in more ways than one. It's a day that God has made, and I'm alive in God's world. I know that all things in my life this day are an expression of God's love—the fact that I'm alive, that I'm recovering, and that I'm able to feel the way I feel at this very instant. For me, this will be a day of gratitude. *Am I deeply thankful for being a part of this special day, and for all my blessings?*

Today I Pray

On this day of remembering God's gift, may I understand that giving and receiving are the same. Each is part of each. If I give, I receive the happiness of giving. If I receive, I give someone else that same happiness of giving. I pray that I may give myself—my love and my strengths—generously. May I also receive graciously the love and strengths of others' selves. May God be our example.

Today I Will Remember

The magnitude of God's giving.

Reflection for the Day

None of us can claim to know God in all His fullness. None of us can really claim to understand our Higher Power to any extent. But this I do know: there is Power beyond my human will which can do wonderful, loving things for me that I can't do for myself. I see this glorious power at work in my own being, and I see the miraculous results of this same power in the lives of thousands upon thousands of other recovering people who are my friends in the Program. *Do I need the grace of God and the loving understanding any less now than when I began my recovery?*

Today I Pray

May I never forget that my spiritual needs are as great today as they were when I came into the Program. It is so easy to look at others, newer to the recovery process, and regard them as the needy ones. As I think of myself as increasingly independent, may I never overlook my dependence on my Higher Power.

Today I Will Remember

I will never outgrow my need for God.

Reflection for the Day

"The central characteristic of the spiritual experience," wrote AA co-founder Bill W., "is that it gives the recipient a new and better motivation out of all proportion to any process of discipline, belief, or faith. These experiences cannot make us whole at once; they are a rebirth to a fresh and certain opportunity." *Do I see my assets as God's gifts, which have been in part matched by an increasing willingness on my part to find and do His will for me?*

Today I Pray

I pray for the wholeness of purpose that can come only through spiritual experience. No amount of intellectual theory, pep-talking to myself, disciplined deprivation, "doing it for" somebody else can accomplish the same results. May I pray for spiritual enlightenment, not only in order to recover, but for itself.

Today I Will Remember

Total motivation through spiritual wholeness.

Reflection for the Day

The Program, for me, is not a place nor a philos-ophy, but a highway to freedom. The highway leads me toward the goal of a "spiritual awaken-ing as the result of these Steps." The highway doesn't get me to the goal as quickly as I some-times wish, but I try to remember that God and I work from different timetables. But the goal is there, and I know that the Twelve Steps will help me reach it. *Have I come to the realization that I and anyone can now do what I had always thought impossible?*

Today I Pray

As I live the Program, may I realize more and more that it is a means to an end rather than an end in itself. May I keep in mind that the kind of spirituality it calls for is never complete, but is the essence of change and growth, a drawing nearer to an ideal state. May I be wary of set-ting time-oriented goals for myself to measure my spiritual progress.

Today I Will Remember

Timetables are human inventions.

Reflection for the Day

The success of the Program, I've been taught, lies in large measure in the readiness and willingness of its members to go to any lengths to help others tyrannized by their addictions. If my readiness and willingness cools, then I stand in danger of losing all that I've gained. I must never become unwilling to give away what I have, for only by so doing will I be privileged to keep it. *Do I take to heart the saying, "Out of self into God into others..."?*

Today I Pray

May I never be too busy to answer a fellow addict s call for help. May I never become so wound up in my pursuits that I forget that my own continuing recovery depends on that helping—a half-hour or so on the telephone, a call in person, a lunch date, whatever the situation calls for. May I know what my priorities must be.

Today I Will Remember

Helping helps me.

Reflection for the Day

My life before coming to the Program was not unlike the lives of so many of us who were cruelly buffeted and tormented by the power of our addictions. For years, I had been sick and tired. When I became sick and tired of being sick and tired, I finally surrendered and came to the Program. Now I realize that I had been helped all along by a Higher Power; it was this Power, indeed, that allowed me to live so that I could eventually find a new way of life. *Since my awakening, have I found a measure of serenity previously unknown in my life?*

Today I Pray

May I realize that my Higher Power has not suddenly come into my life like a stranger opening a door when I knocked. The Power has been there all along, if I will just remember how many brushes with disaster I have survived by a fraction of time or distance. Now that I have come to know my Higher Power better, I realize that I must have been saved for something—for helping others like me.

Today I Will Remember

I am grateful to be alive and recovering

Reflection for the Day

God grant me the SERENITY to accept the things I cannot change; COURAGE to change the things I can; and WISDOM to know the difference—living one day at a time; accepting hardships as the pathway to peace; taking, as He did, this sinful world as it is, not as I would have it; trusting that He will make all things right if I surrender to His Will; that I may be reasonably happy in this life and supremely happy with Him forever in the next. Amen.

Today I Pray

May I look back at this past year as a good one, in that nothing I did or said was wasted. No experience—however insignificant it may have seemed—was worthless. Hurt gave me the capacity to feel happiness; bad times made me appreciate the good ones; what I regarded as my weaknesses became my greatest strengths. I thank God for a year of growing.

Today I Will Remember

Hope is my "balance brought forward"—into a new year's ledger.

THE TWELVE STEPS
OF ALCOHOLICS ANONYMOUS*

1. We admitted we were powerless over alcohol—that our lives had become unmanageable.

2. Came to believe that a Power greater than ourselves could restore us to sanity.

3. Made a decision to turn our will and our lives over to the care of God *as we understood Him.*

4. Made a searching and fearless moral inventory of ourselves.

5. Admitted to God, to ourselves, and to another human being the exact nature of our wrongs.

6. Were entirely ready to have God remove all these defects of character.

7. Humbly asked Him to remove our shortcomings.

8. Made a list of all persons we had harmed, and became willing to make amends to them all.

9. Made direct amends to such people wherever possible, except when to do so would injure them or others.

10. Continued to take personal inventory and when we were wrong promptly admitted it.

11. Sought through prayer and meditation to improve our conscious contact with God *as we understood Him,* praying only for knowledge of His will for us and the power to carry that out.

12. Having had a spiritual awakening as the result of these steps, we tried to carry this message to alcoholics, and to practice these principles in all our affairs.

---

* The Twelve Steps of A.A. are taken from *Alcoholics Anonymous*, 3rd ed., published by A.A. World Services, Inc., New York, N.Y., 59-60. Reprinted with permission of A.A. World Services, Inc.

THE TWELVE TRADITIONS
OF ALCOHOLICS ANONYMOUS*

1. Our common welfare should come first; personal recovery depends upon A.A. unity.

2. For our group purpose there is but one ultimate authority—a loving God as He may express Himself in our group conscience. Our leaders are but trusted servants; they do not govern.

3. The only requirement for A.A. membership is a desire to stop drinking.

4. Each group should be autonomous except in matters affecting other groups or A.A. as a whole.

5. Each group has but one primary purpose—to carry its message to the alcoholic who still suffers.

6. An A.A. group ought never endorse, finance or lend the A.A. name to any related facility or outside enterprise, lest problems of money, property and prestige divert us from our primary purpose.

7. Every A.A. group ought to be fully self-supporting, declining outside contributions.

8. Alcoholics Anonymous should remain forever nonprofessional, but our service centers may employ special workers.

9. A.A., as such, ought never be organized; but we may create service boards or committees directly responsible to those they serve.

10. Alcoholics Anonymous has no opinion on outside issues; hence the A.A. name ought never be drawn into public controversy.

11. Our public relations policy is based on attraction rather than promotion; we need always maintain personal anonymity at the level of press, radio and films.

12. Anonymity is the spiritual foundation of all our Traditions, ever reminding us to place principles before personalities.

---

* The Twelve Traditions of A.A. are taken from *Alcoholics Anonymous*, 3rd ed., published by A.A. World Services, Inc., New York, N.Y. 564. Reprinted with permission of A.A. World Services, Inc.

SUBJECT INDEX

Hazelden, a national nonprofit organization founded in 1949, helps people reclaim their lives from the disease of addiction. Built on decades of knowledge and experience, Hazelden offers a comprehensive approach to addiction that addresses the full range of patient, family, and professional needs, including treatment and continuing care for youth and adults, research, higher learning, public education and advocacy, and publishing.

A life of recovery is lived "one day at a time." Hazelden publications, both educational and inspirational, support and strengthen lifelong recovery. In 1954, Hazelden published *Twenty-Four Hours a Day*, the first daily meditation book for recovering alcoholics, and Hazelden continues to publish works to inspire and guide individuals in treatment and recovery, and their loved ones. Professionals who work to prevent and treat addiction also turn to Hazelden for evidence-based curricula, informational materials, and videos for use in schools, treatment programs, and correctional programs.

Through published works, Hazelden extends the reach of hope, encouragement, help, and support to individuals, families, and communities affected by addiction and related issues.

For questions about Hazelden publications,
please call **800-328-9000**
or visit us online at **hazelden.org/bookstore.**

Other titles of interest...

The Promise of a New Day

by Karen Casey and Martha Vanceburg

This daily guide reaches out to all of us who seek full, healthy living. One page at a time, one day at a time, these meditations guide our path, affirm our strength, and give us a sense of hope and peace. *The Promise of a New Day* is a supportive resource for men and women looking for greater rewards in daily life. 400 pp.

Order No. 1045

Each Day a New Beginning

Daily Meditations for Women

The original meditation classic for women, these 366 daily meditations are enlightening perspectives on self-esteem, relationships, goals, and the power available through a spiritual relationship with a Higher Power. 400 pp.

Order No. 1076

Twenty-Four Hours a Day

Nothing talks like the truth. And nothing tells it better than this classic meditation book. The practice of daily meditation in recovery began with this inspiring resource—still as powerful today as it was 40 years ago. Each day of the year *Twenty-Four Hours a Day* provides an AA Thought for the Day, a short meditation on living the Twelve Step program, and a prayer. 400 pp.

Order No. 5093

For price and order information, or a free catalog,
please call our Telephone Representatives.

HAZELDEN

1-800-328-0098
(Toll Free. U.S.,
Canada, and the
Virgin Islands)

1-651-213-4000
(Outside the U.S.
and Canada)

1-651-257-1331
(24-Hour FAX)

http://www.hazelden.org
(World Wide Web site on Internet)

Pleasant Valley Road • P.O. Box 176 • Center City, MN 55012-0176